Day-by-Day Math Thinking Routines in First Grade

Day-by-Day Math Thinking Routines in First Grade helps you provide students with a review of the foundational ideas in math, every day of the week! Based on the bestselling *Daily Math Thinking Routines in Action*, the book follows the simple premise that frequent, rigorous, engaging practice leads to mastery and retention of concepts, ideas, and skills. These worksheet-free, academically rigorous routines and prompts follow the grade level priority standards and include whole group, individual, and partner work. The book can be used with any math program, or for small groups, workstations, or homework.

Inside you will find:

◆ 40 weeks of practice
◆ 1 activity a day
◆ 200 activities total
◆ Answer Key

For each week, the Anchor Routines cover these key areas: Monday: General Thinking Routines; Tuesday: Vocabulary; Wednesday: Place Value; Thursday: Fluency; and Friday: Problem Solving. Get your students' math muscles moving with the easy-to-follow routines in this book!

Dr. Nicki Newton has been an educator for 30 years, working both nationally and internationally with students of all ages. She has worked on developing Math Workshop and Guided Math Institutes around the country; visit her website at www.drnickinewton.com. She is also an avid blogger (www.guidedmath.wordpress.com), tweeter (@drnickimath) and Pinterest pinner (www.pinterest.com/drnicki7).

Day-by-Day Math Thinking Routines in First Grade

40 Weeks of Quick Prompts and Activities

Dr. Nicki Newton

Routledge
Taylor & Francis Group

NEW YORK AND LONDON

First published 2020
by Routledge
52 Vanderbilt Avenue, New York, NY 10017

and by Routledge
2 Park Square, Milton Park, Abingdon, Oxon, OX14 4RN

Routledge is an imprint of the Taylor & Francis Group, an informa business

Library of Congress Cataloging-in-Publication Data
Names: Newton, Nicki, author.
Title: Day-by-day math thinking routines in first grade : 40 weeks of quick
    prompts and activities / Dr. Nicki Newton.
Description: New York, NY : Routledge, 2020.
Identifiers: LCCN 2019036216 (print) | LCCN 2019036217 (ebook) | ISBN
    9780367421236 (hardback) | ISBN 9780367421229 (paperback) | ISBN
    9780367821944 (ebook)
Subjects: LCSH: Mathematics--Study and teacing (Elementary)--Activity
    programs. | First grade (Education)
Classification: LCC QA135.6 .N48457 2020 (print) | LCC QA135.6 (ebook) |
    DDC 372.7/044--dc23
LC record available at https://lccn.loc.gov/2019036216
LC ebook record available at https://lccn.loc.gov/2019036217

ISBN: 978-0-367-42123-6 (hbk)
ISBN: 978-0-367-42122-9 (pbk)
ISBN: 978-0-367-82194-4 (ebk)

Typeset in Palatino
by Swales & Willis, Exeter, Devon, UK

Contents

Meet the Author

Dr. Nicki Newton has been an educator for 30 years, working both nationally and internationally, with students of all ages. Having spent the first part of her career as a literacy and social studies specialist, she built on those frameworks to inform her math work. She believes that math is intricately intertwined with reading, writing, listening and speaking. She has worked on developing Math Workshop and Guided Math Institutes around the country. Most recently, she has been helping districts and schools nationwide to integrate their State Standards for Mathematics and think deeply about how to teach these within a Math Workshop Model. Dr. Nicki works with teachers, coaches and administrators to make math come alive by considering the powerful impact of building a community of mathematicians who make meaning of real math together. When students do real math, they learn it. They own it, they understand it, and they can do it. Every one of them. Dr. Nicki is also an avid blogger (www. guidedmath.wordpress. com) and Pinterest pinner (https://www.pinterest.com/drnicki7/).

Introduction

Welcome to this exciting new series of daily math thinking routines. I have been doing thinking routines for years. People ask me all the time if I have these written down somewhere. So, I wrote a book. Now, that has turned into a grade level series so that people can do them with prompts that address their grade level standards. This is the anti-worksheet workbook!

The goal is to get students reflecting on their thinking and communicating their mathematical thinking with partners and the whole class about the math they are learning. Marzano (2007)[1] notes that

> initial understanding, albeit a good one, does not suffice for learning that is aimed at long-term retention and use of knowledge. Rather, students must have opportunities to practice new skills and deepen their understanding of new information. Without this type of extended processing, knowledge that students initially understand might fade and be lost over time.

The daily math thinking routines in this book focus on taking Depth of Knowledge activity level 1 activities, to DOK level 2 and 3 activities (Webb, 2002)[2]. Many of the questions are open. For example, we might ask students to tell us a story where the answer is 5 dogs rather than just giving the students a problem to solve. We want students to be comfortable with both open and closed problems (Smalls, 2009)[3].

In this series, we mainly work on priority standards, although we do address some of the supporting and additional standards. This book is not intended to cover every standard. Rather it is meant to provide ongoing daily review of the foundational ideas in math. There is a focus for each day of the week.

- Monday: General Thinking Routines
- Tuesday: Vocabulary
- Wednesday: Place Value
- Thursday: Fluency (American and British Number Talks, Number Strings)
- Friday: Problem Solving

There are general daily thinking routines (What Doesn't Belong?, True or False?, Convince Me!), that review various priority standards from the different domains (Geometry, Algebraic Thinking, Counting, Measurement, Number Sense). Every Tuesday there is an emphasis on Vocabulary because math is a language and if you don't know the words then you can't speak it. There is a continuous review of foundational words through different games (Tic Tac Toe, Match, Bingo), because students need at least 6 encounters with a word to own it. On Wednesday there is often an emphasis on Place Value. Thursday is always some sort of fluency routine (American or British Number Talks and Number Strings). Finally, Fridays are Problem Solving routines.

The book starts with a review of priority and other kindergarten standards and then as the weeks progress the current grade level standards are integrated throughout. There is a heavy

---

1 Marzano, R. J. (2007). *The art and science of teaching: A comprehensive framework for effective instruction.* ASCD: Virginia.
2 Webb, N. (March 28, 2002) "Depth-of-Knowledge Levels for four content areas," unpublished paper.
3 Small, M. (2009). *Good questions: Great ways to differentiate mathematics instruction.* Teachers College Press: New York.

emphasis on work within 10 and Place Value within 120. There is also an emphasis on geometry concepts and some data and measurement. The word problem types for first grade have been woven throughout the year.

Throughout the book there is an emphasis on the mathematical practices/processes (SMP, 2010[4]; NCTM, 2000[5]). Students are expected to problem solve in different ways. They are expected to reason by contextualizing and decontextualizing numbers. They are expected to communicate their thinking to partners and the whole group using the precise mathematical vocabulary. Part of this is reading the work of others, listening to others explanations, writing about their work and then speaking about their work and the work of others in respectful ways. Students are expected to model their thinking with tools and templates. Students are continuously asked to think about the pattern and structure of numbers as they work through the activities.

These activities focus on building mathematical proficiency as defined by the NAP 2001[6]. These activities focus on conceptual understanding, procedural fluency, adaptive reasoning, strategic competence and a student's mathematical disposition. This book can be used with any math program. These are jump starters to the day. They are getting the math muscle moving at the beginning of the day.

Math routines are a form of "guided practice." Marzano notes that although the:

> guided practice is the place where students—working alone, with other students, or with the teacher—engage in the cognitive processing activities of organizing, reviewing, rehearsing, summarizing, comparing, and contrasting. However, it is important that all students engage in these activities. (p. 7)

These are engaging, standards-based, academically rigorous activities that provide meaningful routines that develop mathematical proficiency. The work can also be used for practice with in small groups, workstations and also sent home home as questions for homework.

We have focused on coherence from grade to grade, rigor of thinking, and focus on understanding and being able to explain the math the students are doing. We have intended to take deeper dives into the math, not rushing to the topics of the next grade but going deeper into the topics of the grade at hand (see Figures 1.1–1.4). Here is our criteria for selecting the routines:

◆ Engaging
◆ Easy to learn
◆ Repeatable
◆ Open-ended
◆ Easy to differentiate (adapt and extend for different levels).

4 The Standards of Mathematical Practice. "Common Core State Standards for Mathematical Practice." Washington, D.C.: National Governors Association Center for Best Practices, Council of Chief State School Officers, 2010. Retrieved on December 1, 2019 from: www.corestandards.org/Math/Practice.

5 National Council of Teachers of Mathematics. (2000). *Principles and standards for school mathematics*. Reston, VA: National Council of Teachers of Mathematics.

6 Kilpatrick, J., Swafford, J., and Findell, B. (eds.) (2001). *Adding it up: Helping children learn mathematics*. Washington, DC: National Academy Press.

Figure 1.1 Talking about the Routine!

Monday: General Thinking Routines

3 + ___ = 7

Jen said that the answer is 10. Kelly said the answer is 4. Who do you agree with? Why?

Tuesday: Vocabulary

difference	subtract
addend	take away

Wednesday: Guess My Number

I am a 2 digit number.
I am more than 12.
I am less than 20.
My digits add up to 9.
Who am I?

Thursday: Number Strings

7 + 4
7 + 5
7 + 6
7 + 7

Friday: Make Your Own Problem

Mike had _____ marbles. He gave _____away. How many did he have left?
    (4 or 5)   (1, 2 or 3)

Figure 1.2 The Math Routine Cycle of Engagement

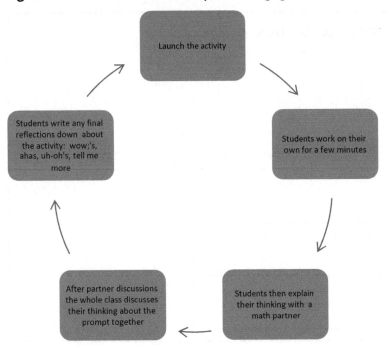

Step 1: Students are given the launch prompt. The teacher explains the prompt and makes sure that everyone understands what they are working on.

Step 2: They are given a few minutes to work on that prompt by themselves.

Step 3: The next step is for students to work with a math partner. As they work with this partner, students are expected to listen to what their partner did as well as explain their own work.

Step 4: Students come back together as a whole group and discuss the math. They are encouraged to talk about how they solved it and the similarities and differences between their thinking and their partner's thinking.

Step 5: Students reflect on the prompt of the day, thinking about what Wowed them, what made them say ah-ha, what made them say uh-oh, what made them say, "I need to know more about this."

Thinking Activities

These are carefully planned practice activities to get students to think. They are **not meant to be used as a workbook**. This is a thinking activity book. The emphasis is on students doing their own work, explaining what they did with a partner and then sharing out to the entire class.

Overview of the Routines

Monday Routines – General Thinking Routines (Algebraic Thinking, Measurement, Data, Geometry)

- Always, Sometimes, Never
- Convince Me!
- Graphs
- How Many More to
- Leg and Feet Problems
- Magic Square
- Missing Hundred Grid
- Reasoning Matrices
- Reasoning Missing Numbers
- 3 Truths and a Fib
- True or False?
- 2 Arguments
- What Doesn't Belong?

Tuesday Routines – Vocabulary

- Alike and Different
- Frayer Model
- Graphs
- It Is/It Isn't
- Vocabulary Bingo
- Vocabulary Brainstorm
- Vocabulary Fill-in
- Vocabulary Match
- Vocabulary Quick-Write
- Vocabulary Talk
- Vocabulary Tic Tac Toe
- What Doesn't Belong?

Wednesday Routines – Place Value

- Alike and Different
- Compose It!
- Convince Me!
- Greater Than, Less Than, in Between
- Guess My Number
- How Many More to
- Magic Square
- Missing Numbers
- Number Bond It!
- Number Line it!
- Number of the Day
- What Doesn't Belong?

Thursday Routines – Number Talk

♦ Number Talk
♦ Number Strings

Friday Routines – Problem Solving

♦ Equation Match
♦ Make Your Own Problem
♦ Match the Model
♦ Model It
♦ Picture That!
♦ What's the Problem?
♦ What's the Story?
♦ What's the Question? (3 Read Protocol)

Figure 1.3 Overview of the Routines

Routine	Purpose	Description
Always, Sometimes, Never	Students should be able to reason about mathematical statements.	Students have to discuss whether a statement is always, sometimes or never true.
Composing Numbers	Composing and decomposing numbers is a stepping stone to adding and subtracting.	Students use ten frames to compose and decompose different numbers.
Convince Me!	This routine focuses on students reasoning about different topics. They have to convince their peers about specific statements.	Students are given different things to think about like statements or equations and they have to convince their peers that they are correct.
Equation Match	This routine focuses on students thinking about which operation they would use to solve a problem. It requires that they reason about the actions that are happening in the problem and then what they are required to do to solve the problem.	Students are trying to match the word problem and the equation.
Frayer Model	This routine is meant to get students talking about concepts. They are supposed to talk about the definition, what happens in real life, sketch an example and also give non-examples.	Students are given a template with labels. They work through the template writing and drawing about the specified topic.
Graphs	Students should know how to read and interpret data.	Students have to read the information and then make a graph based on that information and ask questions about the information.
Guess My Number	This routine gives students a variety of clues about a number and asks the students to guess which number it might be given all the clues. Students have to use their understanding of place value and math vocabulary to figure out which number is being discussed.	In this routine, students are given various clues about a number and they must use the clues to guess which number it is.
How Many More to	In this routine, students are asked to tell how many to a specific number. Again, this is another place value routine, asking students to reason about numbers on the number line.	In this routine, students are given a specific number and they have to tell how many more to the target number.

Routine	Purpose	Description
It Is/It Isn't	This routine can be used in a variety of ways. Students have to look at the topic and decide what it is and what it isn't. It is another way of looking at the concept of example, non-example.	In this routine, students discuss what something is and what it isn't.
Legs and Feet	Legs and feet is a great arithmetic routine which gets students to use various operations to figure out how many animals there are by working with numbers.	Students look at different animals and think about how many legs and feet there could be given that number of animals.
Magic Square	This routine works on addition fact power.	There are 2 ways to work with Magic Squares. The first way is to figure out what is the "magic sum." To figure out the magic sum, the answer must be the same when totaling the numbers in all directions. The second way to play is to fill in numbers to get a given "magic sum". Again, the missing numbers are placed in a way that they make the "magic sum" in all directions.
Make Your Own Problem	In this word problem routine students get to pick their own numbers to create and then solve a word problem.	Students fill in the blanks with numbers to make their own problems.
Match the Model	In this word problem routine, students have to find the word problem that matches the model. It is another way to work on the representation of word problems.	Students are trying to match the word problem and the model.
Missing Numbers in a Number Line	Students should know the sequence of numbers.	Students have to fill in the missing numbers on the number path.
Missing Numbers in an Equation	Students should be able to reason about equations.	Students fill in missing numbers in an equation.
Missing Numbers in a Hundred Grid	Students should understand and use place value to fill in the number grid.	Students have to figure out what is missing in the empty squares of a hundred grid.
Model It	In this word problem routine, students are focusing on representing word problems in a variety of ways.	Students have to represent their thinking about a word problem with various models.

Routine	Purpose	Description
Number Bond It!	In this routine, students are working on decomposing numbers in a variety of ways.	Students use number bonds to break apart numbers in different ways.
Number of the Day	This activity focuses on students modeling numbers in a variety of ways.	This activity has a given number and students have to represent that number in different ways.
Number Line It!	This activity focuses on sequencing numbers correctly.	Students have to put numbers in the correct sequence on the number path or number line.
Number Talk	This activity focuses on number sense. Students compose and decompose numbers as well as add and subtract numbers.	There are a few different ways that students do this activity. One of the ways is the teacher works with the students on showing a number in a variety of ways. Another activity is that the teacher gives the students Number Strings around a specific concept for example subtracting 1 from a number and students work those problems and discuss the strategy.
Number Strings	In this routine, students are looking at the relationship among a set of problems.	Students work out the different problems and think about and discuss the various strategies they are using.
Reasoning Matrices	Reasoning Matrices help students to reason about information and decide what makes sense given that information.	In this routine, students are given information about children and they have to decide which information matches which child.
3 Truths and a Fib	Students should reason about mathematical statements.	In this routine, students are given 4 statements. Three statements are true and one is false. Students have to decide which one is false.
True or False?	This activity focuses on students reasoning about what is true or false.	Students are given different things to think about like statements about shapes or equations and they have to state and prove whether they are true or false.
2 Arguments	In this reasoning routine, students are thinking about common errors that students make when doing various math tasks like missing numbers, working with properties and working with the equal sign.	Students listen to the way 2 different students approached a problem, decide who they agreed with and defend their thinking.

Routine	Purpose	Description
Vocabulary Bingo	This activity focuses on vocabulary.	Students play Bingo. Teachers will need to make copies of the boards for students. Or the students can play it in teams as a class on the board.
Vocabulary Brainstorm	This activity focuses on vocabulary.	Students brainstorm about math vocabulary. They can brainstorm using words, pictures, and numbers.
Vocabulary Match	Students should understand and know how to use math vocabulary.	In this routine, students match the vocabulary words with definitions and/or pictures.
Vocabulary Greater Than, Less Than, in Between	Students should understand the relationship of numbers to each other on the number line.	Students have to discuss number relationships given specific numbers.
Vocabulary Talk	Students discuss vocabulary words.	In this activity, students discuss 1 or 2 words in a conversation.
Vocabulary Tic Tac Toe	Students should be able to name and use math vocabulary.	Students have to discuss the words with their partner. They have to draw or write or explain their thinking before they put the x or o. Whoever gets 3 in a row first wins. Teachers will need to make copies of the boards for students. Or the students can play it in teams as a class on the board.
Vocabulary Alike and Different	This activity focuses on students reasoning about what is the same and what is different with objects.	Students are shown 2 or 3 different things and they have to discuss how they are alike and different.
Vocabulary Fill-in	Students focus on vocabulary.	Students read the sentences and fill in the missing words.
Vocabulary Quick-Write	Students need to know math vocabulary.	In this activity they write down everything they can about a given word. They can use numbers, words and pictures.
What Doesn't Belong?	This is a reasoning activity where students have to choose which objects they can group together and why. The emphasis is on justification.	Students have 4 squares. They have to figure out which object does not belong.

Routine	Purpose	Description
What's the Story?/Picture That!	Students should be able to tell a story when given objects or a picture.	In this routine, students are shown a picture and they have to tell what is happening in the story.
What's the Problem?	Students should be able to contextualize numbers.	In this routine students are given an equation and they have to choose the problem that matches the equation.
What's the Question?	Students should be able to reason about a story context.	Students are given a story context and they have to come up with questions about that context.

Questioning Is the Key 🔑

To Unlock the Magic of Thinking, You Need Good Questions!

Figure 1.4

Launch Questions (Before the Activity)	Process Questions (During the Activity)
◆ What is this prompt asking us to do? ◆ How will you start? ◆ What are you thinking? ◆ Explain to your math partner, your understanding of the question. ◆ What will you do to solve this problem?	◆ What will you do first? ◆ How will you organize your thinking? ◆ What might you do to get started? ◆ What is your strategy? ◆ Why did you….? ◆ Why are you doing that? ◆ Is that working? Does it make sense? ◆ Is that a reasonable answer? ◆ Can you prove it? ◆ Are you sure about that answer? ◆ How do you know you are correct?
Debrief Questions (After the Activity)	**Partner Questions (Guide Student Conversations)**
◆ What did you do? ◆ How did you get your answer? ◆ How do you know it is correct? ◆ Can you prove it? ◆ Convince me that you have the correct answer ◆ Is there another way to think about this problem?	◆ Tell me what you did. ◆ Tell me more about your model. ◆ Tell me more about your drawing. ◆ Tell me more about your calculations. ◆ Tell me more about your thinking. ◆ Can you prove it? ◆ How do you know you are right? ◆ I understand what you did. ◆ I don't understand what you did yet.

Daily Routines

Week 1 Teacher Notes

Monday: What Doesn't Belong?

When introducing this routine, the teacher should work with the students to solve each box and then decide which one doesn't belong.

Tuesday: Alike and Different

Students should be able to discuss how the shapes are alike with sides that are closed, how they have points (vertices) and how the sides are straight. We want to focus on the attributes of the shapes.

Wednesday: Number Bond It!

This is an opportunity for students to build on their work on composing and decomposing numbers to 10.

Thursday: Number Talk

This is an opportunity for students to work on adding 1 to a number. They should talk about how you just have to think of the next number.

Friday: What's the Story?

You want students to act this out and then discuss the pictures.

Week 1 Activities

Monday: What Doesn't Belong?

Look at the options in each box. Figure out which one doesn't belong. Decide and discuss.

A.

2 + 3	5 – 0
4 + 2	1 + 4

B.

5 – 2	6 – 3
7 – 5	1 + 1 + 1

Tuesday: Alike and Different

Look at the shapes and decide and discuss how they are alike and how they are different.

Wednesday: Number Bond It!

Fill in the missing numbers.

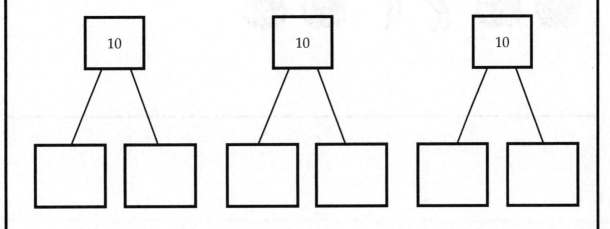

Thursday: Number Talk

What are some ways to think about:

2 + 1
3 + 1
4 + 1
7 + 1

What happens when you add 1 to a number?

1	2	3	4	5	6	7	8	9	10

Friday: What's the Story?

Tell a story about these pictures.

Week 2 Teacher Notes

Monday: True or False?

In this routine the students discuss whether or not statements are true or false. Here they are working with the number 0. It is important for students to be able to explain what is happening when they are working with 0.

Tuesday: It Is/It Isn't

In this routine students are describing the number 16. They have to discuss what it is and what it isn't. For example, it is a 2 digit number. It is greater than 15. It isn't a 1 digit number. It isn't greater than 20.

Wednesday: Number Line It!

Students have to discuss how to order and plot the numbers on the number line from least to greatest.

Thursday: Number Talk

Students work on adding numbers within 10. They have to discuss whether or not they did it in their head, with a drawing or on paper.

Friday: Model It

Students act out the word problems and then discuss the pictorial representation.

Week 2 Activities

Monday: True or False?

Look at the boxes. Decide and discuss whether the equation is true or false.

A. $2 + 0 = 0$

B. $3 + 0 = 3$

C. $4 - 0 = 0$

D. $2 - 0 = 2$

Tuesday: It Is/It Isn't

Describe what the number is and what it isn't.

16

It Is	It Isn't

Word bank: Greater Than, Less Than, in Between, 1 digit, 2 digit, ones, tens.

Wednesday: Number Line It!

Think about and discuss the order of numbers with your math partner. Line them up from least to greatest on the number line.

2   7   3   5   9

0   10

Thursday: Number Talk

Pick a number from each circle Then decide how you are going to add them. Write the problem under the way you solved it. For example, 8 + 2. I can do that in my head because it is a ten friend.

Can I do it in my head?	Did I use a model?	Did I write down the numbers and solve it on paper?

Circle 1: 1 2 0 3 4 5

Circle 2: 1 2 0 3 4 5

Friday: Model It

Solve on the number line.

Sue had 5 marbles. She got 1 more. How many does she have now?

Week 3 Teacher Notes

Monday: Missing Numbers

Students have to fill in the missing numbers on the number path.

Tuesday: Vocabulary Talk

Students have to discuss different teen numbers.

Wednesday: Number of the Day

Students have to fill in the boxes to represent the number ten. Have the students do it on their own, discuss with a partner and then debrief with the whole class.

Thursday: Number Talk

Students work on solving the problem in different ways.

Friday: What's the Story?

Students have to come up with a problem to match the expression. They discuss it, then draw a picture and represent it in the ten frame.

Week 3 Activities

Monday: Missing Numbers

Fill in the missing numbers.

10			14							20

Tuesday: Vocabulary Talk

Name 3 teen numbers!

Write them.

Wednesday: Number of the Day

Look at the number and fill in the boxes to match the number.

10

Number word	Ten frame

Write the number.

Thursday: Number Talk

What are some ways we can make 7? Think about ways using addition or subtraction.

Friday: What's the Story?

$$2 + 2$$

Tell a story.

Draw a picture	Ten frame

Week 4 Teacher Notes

Monday: 2 Arguments

Students have to discuss and decide who is correct. They need to defend their thinking with a partner. This is an opportunity to discuss the meaning of the equal sign.

Tuesday: It Is/It Isn't

Students have to describe what a square is and what it isn't. They can talk about how it is a closed figure with 4 sides, 4 vertices and 4 angles. They can say it isn't curved. It isn't a circle. It isn't open.

Wednesday: How Many More to

Students have to reason about numbers. They need to know how many more to a given number.

Thursday: Number Talk

Students discuss what happens when you take away 1 from a number. They should discuss how it is the number before.

Friday: Picture That!

Students have to tell a story about the fruits. They can tell an addition or subtraction story. They should write a number sentence as well.

Week 4 Activities

Monday: 2 Arguments

Discuss and decide who is correct. Defend your thinking to your partner.

$7 + \underline{} = 7$

John said the answer is 0.

Mike said the answer is 14.

Who do you agree with?

Why?

Prove it!

Tuesday: It Is/It Isn't

Describe what the word is and what it isn't.

Square

It Is	It Isn't

Word bank: corners (vertices), straight lines, sides, shape, same as, round.

Wednesday: How Many More to

Use the number path to help you! How many more to 10?

Start at 0
Start at 1
Start at 3
Start at 7
Start at 4
Start at 9
Start at 2

1	2	3	4	5	6	7	8	9	10

Thursday: Number Talk

What happens when you subtract 1 from a number?

4 − 1 = 3

3 − 1 = 2

7 − 1 = 6

What happens when you take away 1 from a number?

0 ← ─────────────────────────────── → 10

Friday: Picture That!

Tell a story about these fruits.

Story:
Number Sentence:

Week 5 Teacher Notes

Monday: True or False?

In this routine the students discuss whether or not statements are true or false.

Tuesday: Vocabulary Match

Students have to match the word with the correct definition.

Wednesday: Number of the Day

Students represent numbers in a variety of ways.

Thursday: Number Talk

Students work on adding numbers within 10. They have to discuss whether or not they did it in their head, with a drawing, or on paper.

Friday: Make Your Own Problem

Students have to fill in the numbers and discuss the problem.

Monday: True or False?

Look at the boxes. Decide and discuss whether the statement is true or false.

A. 8 is greater than 9.
B. 10 is less than 20.
C. 100 is more than 12.
D. 5 is less than 4.

Tuesday: Vocabulary Match

Match the word with the correct shape.

circle	▬	
square	⬡	
rectangle	●	
hexagon	▮	
trapezoid	◿	
triangle	⏢	

Wednesday: Number of the Day

Look at the number and fill in the boxes to match the number.

14

Write the number.

Circle it on the number line.

1	2	3	4	5	6	7	8	9	10	11	12	13	14	15	16	17	18	19	20

Model it in the twenty frame.

Fill in the missing numbers.

11	12			15	16			19	

Thursday: Number Talk

Pick a number from each circle. Then, decide how you are going to add the numbers. Write the problem under the way you solved it. For example, 5 + 5. I can do that in my head because it is a ten friend.

Did I do it in my head?	Did I use a model?	Did I write down the numbers and solve it on paper?

1 2 3 4 5   1 2 3 4 5

Friday: Make Your Own Problem

Ray had _____ marbles. He got _____ more for his

      4 or 5   1 or 2

birthday. Now, he has _____.

Model it.

Number sentence (equation): _____

Week 6 Teacher Notes

Monday: Always, Sometimes, Never

Students discuss and decide if this statement is always, sometime or never true!

Tuesday: Alike and Different

Students should be able to discuss how the solids are alike and different. We want them to focus on the attributes of the solids.

Wednesday: How Many More to

Students have to reason about numbers. They need to know how many more to a given number.

Thursday: Number Talk

In this number talk, students talk about taking a number from itself. They look at and discuss the pattern.

Friday: Model It

Students solve the problem in more than 1 way.

Week 6 Activities

Monday: Always, Sometimes, Never

Discuss and decide if this statement is always, sometime or never true!

1st graders are taller than kindergarteners.

Tuesday: Alike and Different

Look at the solids and decide and discuss how they are alike and how they are different.

Word bank: 2D shapes, 3D shapes, roll, straight side, curved side, flat side, flat, round, vertex.

Wednesday: How Many More to

Start at 5 … how many more to 10?

1	2	3	4	5					

Start at 7 … how many more to 10?

1	2	3	4	5	6	7			

Start at 3 … how many more to 10?

1	2	3							

Thursday: Number Talk

2 − 2
3 − 3
4 − 4
5 − 5
8 − 8

What happens when we take away a number from itself?

Friday: Model It

Jan had 2 marbles. She got 8 more. How many does she have now?

_____ + _____ =

Picture

Ten Frame

Week 7 Teacher Notes

Monday: What Doesn't Belong?

In this routine students have to discuss what shape doesn't belong and why.

Tuesday: Alike and Different

Students should be able to discuss how the shapes are alike with sides that are closed, how they have points (vertices) and how the sides are straight. We want to focus on the attributes of the shapes.

Wednesday: Number Bond It!

Students practice decomposing 7 in different ways.

Thursday: Number Talk

Students have to discuss what happens when you take 0 from a number.

Friday: Problem Solving

Students solve the problem and model it in a part-part whole diagram and on a number path.

Monday: What Doesn't Belong?

Look at the options in each box. Figure out which one doesn't belong. Decide and discuss.

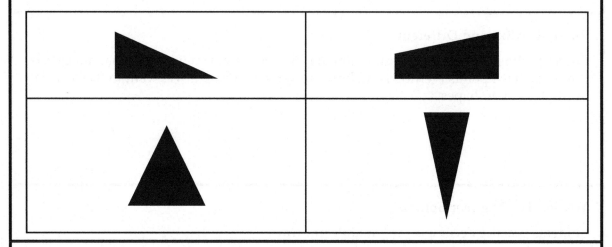

Tuesday: Alike and Different

Look at the shapes and decide and discuss how they are alike and how they are different.

Word bank: sides, angles, corners (vertices) straight, polygons, number of sides.

Wednesday: Number Bond It!

Fill in the empty boxes.

Ways to make 7.

7	7	7
6 ☐	☐ 5	☐ ☐

Thursday: Number Talk

What happens when you subtract 0 from a number? Give some examples.

Friday: Problem Solving

Mark had 2 big marbles and 3 small ones. How many did he have altogether?

Whole	
Part	Part

1	2	3	4	5	6	7	8	9	10

Week 8 Teacher Notes

Monday: True or False?

In this routine the students discuss whether or not this figure is a hexagon. They should reason outloud.

Tuesday: It Is/It Isn't

Students have to describe what a rectangle is and isn't. For example, it is a shape, with closed straight sides. It isn't a curved shape.

Wednesday: Number Bond It!

This is an opportunity for students to build on their work on composing and decomposing numbers to 9.

Thursday: Number Talk

This is an opportunity for students to work on subtraction from numbers up to 5.

Friday: Model It

Students work on representing word problems in different ways.

Monday: True or False?

Look at the boxes. Decide and discuss whether the statement is true or false.

This is a hexagon.

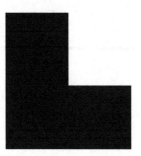

1. Think about it.
2. Share your thinking with a friend. Defend your answer.
3. Share your thinking with the group.

Tuesday: It Is/It Isn't

Describe what the word is and what it isn't.

Rectangle

It Is	It Isn't

Wednesday: Number Bond It!

Show how to break apart 9 in 3 different ways!

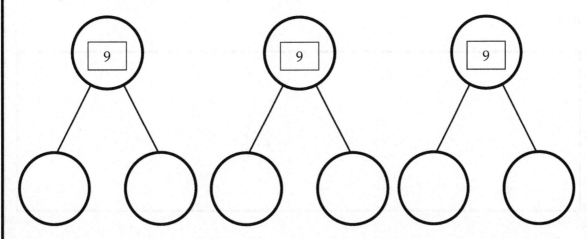

Thursday: Number Talk

Pick a number from each circle. Make a subtraction problem. Write the problem under the way you solved it.

For example: 5 − 1 = 4.

Did I do it in my head?	Did I use a model?	Did I write down the numbers and solve it on paper?

A.

5 4 3

B.

0 1 2

Friday: Model It

Jamal had 7 marbles. He gave 2 to Mike. How many did he have left?

Picture

Ten Frame

Write the Equation   _____ − _____ = _____

Week 9 Teacher Notes

Monday: Convince Me!

Students reason about an equation. They should use numbers, words and pictures to justify their answers.

Tuesday: Vocabulary Talk

Students discuss the words compose and decompose.

Wednesday: Guess My Number

Students use the clues to guess the number. They can use number lines and number grids to help them.

Thursday: Number Strings

Students discuss what the pattern is that they see in these expressions. The discussion should focus on counting back 1, 2, or 3.

Friday: What's the Story?

Students work on telling and representing word problems in different ways.

Week 9 Activities

Monday: Convince Me!

Convince me that:

$4 + 6 = 10$

Use numbers, words and pictures.

Tuesday: Vocabulary Talk

Discuss as a class.

What do the words compose and decompose mean? Let's talk about it and give examples.

Wednesday: Guess My Number

Use the clues to guess the number. Look at the number path to help you figure out the number.

1	2	3	4	5	6	7	8	9	10

My number is greater than $2 + 2$.

My number is less than $10 - 3$.

My number is the sum of a doubles fact.

Thursday: Number Strings

Discuss the problems and talk about how to solve them.

10 – 1
9 – 2
8 – 3
7 – 2
6 – 1
5 – 3

When and how do we use the "count back" strategy?

Friday: What's the Story?

Make up a story about this picture.

Week 10 Teacher Notes

Monday: Convince Me!

Students have to convince the class that there are many ways to make and model the number 8. They should do it with their math partner and then share it outloud to the group.

Tuesday: Vocabulary Talk

Students should discuss the words sum and difference.

Wednesday: Number of the Day

Students have to fill in the boxes to represent the number 17. Have the students do it on their own, discuss with a partner and then debrief with the whole class.

Thursday: Number Talk

The focus of this conversation should be on doubles.

Friday: What's the Question? (3 Read Protocol)

Read the problem stem 3 times. The first time read it and ask about the context. The second time read it and talk about the numbers. The third time read it and ask what questions could be asked about the scenario. The teacher records these questions on the board. Then give the students time to think about the answers and discuss them.

Week 10 Activities

Monday: Convince Me!

Convince me that there are many ways to make and model the number 8.

Tuesday: Vocabulary Talk

Discuss as a class.

What do the words sum and difference mean? Let's talk about it and give examples.

Wednesday: Number of the Day

17

Write the Number	Part-Part Whole	Twenty Frame
Circle the ones that make 17 $8 + 9$ $17 + 0$ $5 + 5$ $10 + 17$	Solve: $17 + ? = 18$ $17 - ? = 16$	How many more to 20?
Twenty Frame		

Thursday: Number Talk

Discuss:

1 + 1   2 + 2   3 + 3   4 + 4   5 + 5

Friday: What's the Question? (3 Read Protocol)

Maya had 5 yellow crayons, 2 green ones and 3 blue ones.

What are some possible questions?

Monday: Reasoning Matrices

Students have to reason about the information given to them and then decide which child matches the description.

Tuesday: Vocabulary Bingo

Students listen for their numbers and then cover 1 number at a time. Whoever gets 4 in a row, across, up or down or diagonally wins. The focus here is on teen numbers. Teachers should call out the numbers, discuss the tens and ones, show pictures that represent that number and show the number.

Wednesday: Greater Than, Less Than, in Between

Students have to discuss the relationship of numbers. They work on using the language of comparison as well.

Thursday: Number Talk

Students practice making subtraction problems within 10. They have to discuss how they solved them.

Friday: Problem Solving

Students are working on decomposing the number 5 with pictures. This is a kindergarten standard but most first graders are still working on this concept. Students should be able to represent the number in all the different ways.

Monday: Reasoning Matrices

Who ate which cookie?

Sue does not like sprinkles but she loves chips. Carl does not like chocolate. Lucy will eat any of the cookies.

Sue			
Carl			
Lucy			

Tuesday: Vocabulary Bingo

Teen numbers
11, 12, 13, 14, 15, 16, 17, 18, 19
As your teacher calls a number, cover it. One number at a time.
Cover a number less than. Cover a number with ___ tens.
Cover a number equal to. Cover a number with ____ ones.
Cover a number with _____ tens and _____ones.
Cover a number in between _____ and _____.

11	19	12	13
17	13	16	15
13	15	19	14
15	12	11	18

15	12	18	14
11	13	16	19
17	14	15	17
13	18	12	11

Wednesday: Greater, Less Than, in Between

Fill in the boxes based on these numbers.

3, 10, 20

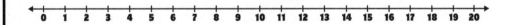

What is a number that is greater than 3?	What is a number that is less than 10?	What is a number that is greater than 20?
What is a number that is less than 3?	What is a number that is in between 3 and 10?	What is a number that is in between 10 and 20?

Thursday: Number Talk

Pick a number from each circle. Make a subtraction problem. Write the problem under the way you solved it. For example, 8 – 7. I did it on my fingers. I held up 8 and put down 7. I had 1 left.

Did I do it in my head?	Did I use a model?	Did I write down the numbers and solve it on paper?

A.

```
8     4    2
6   5      7
```

B.

```
5
        6    4
7       1       2
```

Friday: Problem Solving

In the barnyard there were chickens and cows. There was a total of 5 animals. How many different combinations could there be if there has to be at least 1 chicken and a (1) cow?

Fill out the rest of the chart!

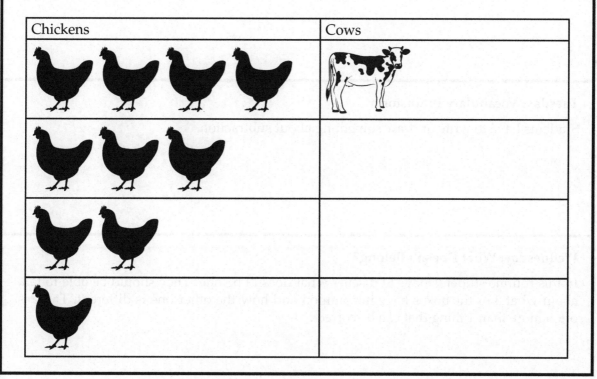

Chickens	Cows

Week 12 Teacher Notes

Monday: Legs and Feet

Students have to reason about how many legs there are, given the animals.

Tuesday: Vocabulary Brainstorm

Students have to write or draw something about subtraction.

Wednesday: What Doesn't Belong?

In this routine students have to discuss what doesn't belong. They should be able to talk about what 3 of the boxes have in common and how the other one is different. There is often more than 1 thing that can be correct.

Thursday: Number Talk

Students discuss a variety of ways to solve and model 10 - 8.

Friday: Equation Match

Students have to match the problem with the equation.

Monday: Legs and Feet

There is a chicken and a cow.

A. How many legs?

B. If there are 10 legs and there has to be a chicken and a cow, how many animals and what type are there?

Way 1	Way 2

Tuesday: Vocabulary Brainstorm

In each thought cloud write or draw something that has to do with subtraction.

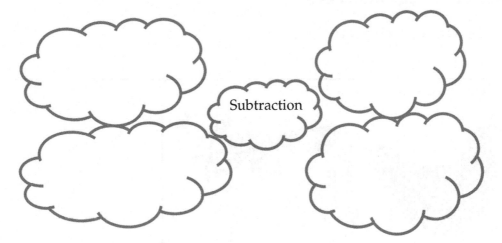

Subtraction

Wednesday: What Doesn't Belong?

Look at the options in each box. Figure out which one doesn't belong. Decide and discuss.

25	2 tens 5 ones
25 ones	25 − 1

Thursday: Number Talk

What are some ways to subtract 10 − 8?

Friday: Equation Match

Match the story with the correct equation.

Jim had 4 marbles. He got some more. Now he has 10. How many did he get?

1. $4 + \square = 10$
2. $\square + 4 = 10$
3. $10 - \square = 4$
4. None of the above.

Week 13 Teacher Notes

Monday: What Doesn't Belong?

In this routine students have to discuss what doesn't belong. They should be able to talk about what 3 of the boxes have in common and how the other one is different. There is often more than 1 thing that can be correct.

Tuesday: Frayer Model

Students have to discuss the word. Fill in the boxes to describe and give examples of the word.

Wednesday: Compose It!

Students have to use 2 different crayons (colors) to show 4 ways to make the number 6 on the models below. They should do it, explain their thinking to a partner and then discuss their ways with the class.

Thursday: Number Talk

Students should be looking at the pattern and noticing and discussing what happens when neighbor numbers are subtracted.

Friday: What's the Story?

Students work on telling and modeling word problems with different tools.

Monday: What Doesn't Belong?

Look at the options in each box. Figure out which one doesn't belong. Decide and discuss.

A.

add	difference
total	altogether

B.

$3 + 2 + 3$	$1 + 3 + 3$
$4 + 2 + 1$	$10 - 3$

Tuesday: Frayer Model

Discuss the word. Fill in the boxes to describe and give examples of the word.

Equation

Definition	Examples
When Do You Use Them?	Non-examples

Wednesday: Compose It!

Use 2 different crayons (colors) to show 4 ways to make the number 6 on the models below.

Explain your thinking to a partner. Be ready to share your thinking with the whole class.

Thursday: Number Talk

What are some strategies and models to think about and show:

8 – 7
7 – 6
5 – 4
3 – 2

What do you notice about all these problems?

Friday: What's the Story?

Use the pictures to write a story problem.

Story:

Model:

Equation:

Week 14 Teacher Notes

Monday: Always, Sometimes, Never

Students have to listen to the statement and then discuss and decide if this statement is always, sometimes or never true!

Tuesday: Vocabulary Bingo

Students listen for the shapes and then cover 1 shape at a time. The teacher should call out attributes as well as the name of shapes. For example: cover a shape that has three sides. Or, cover a triangle.

Wednesday: Guess My Number

Students use the clues to guess the number. They can use number lines and number grids to help them.

Thursday: Number Talk

Students discuss doubles facts.

Friday: What's the Story?

Students work on telling and solving word problems with a variety of models.

Week 14 Activities

Monday: Always, Sometimes, Never

Discuss and decide if this statement is always, sometime or never true.

When you subtract the number always gets smaller.

Tuesday: Vocabulary Bingo

Pick a board. Cover 1 shape at a time. Whoever gets 4 in a row, across, up or down or diagonally wins.

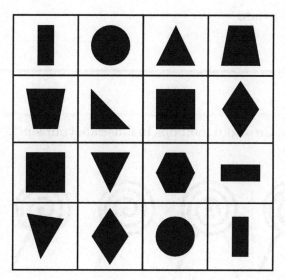 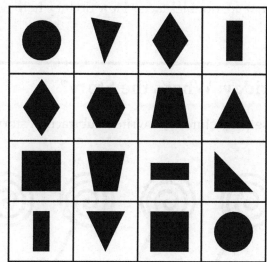

Wednesday: Guess My Number

Use the clues to guess the number.

1	2	3	4	5	6	7	8	9	10
11	12	13	14	15	16	17	18	19	20
21	22	23	24	25	26	27	28	29	30
31	32	33	34	35	36	37	38	39	40
41	42	43	44	45	46	47	48	49	50
51	52	53	54	55	56	57	58	59	60
61	62	63	64	65	66	67	68	69	70
71	72	73	74	75	76	77	78	79	80
81	82	83	84	85	86	87	88	89	90
91	92	93	94	95	96	97	98	99	100

Look at the hundred grid to help you figure out the number.

A.	B.
I am a 2 digit number.	I am a 2 digit number.
I am greater than 15.	I am less than 30.
I am less than 20.	I am greater than 20.
My ones digit is the sum of 4 + 4.	My ones digit is the sum of 4 + 3.
Who am I?	Who am I?

Thursday: Number Talk

What are doubles facts? How do they help us to add?

Friday: What's the Story?

Use the pictures and write a subtraction story. Cross out lollipops to illustrate your story.

Story:

Model:

Equation:

Week 15 Teacher Notes

Monday: How Many More to

Students have to reason about numbers. They need to know how many more to a given number.

Tuesday: Vocabulary Fill-in

Students have to use the words in the word bank to fill in the blanks.

Wednesday: What Doesn't Belong?

In this routine students have to discuss what doesn't belong. They should be able to talk about what 3 of the boxes have in common and how the other one is different. There is often more than 1 thing that can be correct.

Thursday: Number Strings

Students discuss what happens when we subtract 10 from a number.

Friday: Problem Solving

Students read and solve the problem using the diagram.

Monday: How Many More to

Look at the number path to help you think about how many more to 12.

1	2	3	4	5	6	7	8	9	10

Start at 2
Start at 3
Start at 4
Start at 5
Start at 7

Tuesday: Vocabulary Fill-in

Use the words in the word bank to fill in the blanks below.

Word bank: difference, sum, addend.

A. The answer to an addition problem is called the _____.

B. The answer to a subtraction problem is called the _____.

C. The number in an addition problem is called _____.

Wednesday: What Doesn't Belong?

Look at the options in each box. Figure out which one doesn't belong. Decide and Discuss.

A.

15 − 7	4 + 4
14 − 7	2 + 3 + 3

B.

5 + 6	7 + 4
8 + 3	9 + 1

Thursday: Number Strings

What are some ways to think about and show:

10 – 10
20 – 10
30 – 10
40 – 10
50 – 10

1	2	3	4	5	6	7	8	9	10
11	12	13	14	15	16	17	18	19	20
21	22	23	24	25	26	27	28	29	30
31	32	33	34	35	36	37	38	39	40
41	42	43	44	45	46	47	48	49	50
51	52	53	54	55	56	57	58	59	60
61	62	63	64	65	66	67	68	69	70
71	72	73	74	75	76	77	78	79	80
81	82	83	84	85	86	87	88	89	90
91	92	93	94	95	96	97	98	99	100

Friday: Problem Solving

Mary had 8 rings. Some were blue and 3 were red. How many were blue?

A.

Whole	
Part	Part

B.   Equation (write an equation with a symbol for the part we are looking for).

Week 16 Teacher Notes

Monday: Reasoning Matrices

Students have to reason about the information given to them and then decide which child matches the description.

Tuesday: Vocabulary Bingo

Students listen for their numbers and then cover 1 number at a time. Whoever gets 4 in a row, across, up or down or diagonally wins

Wednesday: Missing Numbers

Students have to fill in the missing numbers in the hundred grid.

Thursday: Number Talk

Students work on adding numbers within 18. They have to discuss whether or not they did it in their head, with a drawing or on paper with calculations.

Friday: Model It

Students work on word problems using a variety of models.

Monday: Reasoning Matrices

Carl loves a game where you kick and hold the ball. Lucy loves a game where you mainly kick the ball and do head tricks. Sue likes a game where you have to use a bat. Which ball did each student have?

Sue			
Carl			
Lucy			

Tuesday: Vocabulary Bingo

As your teacher calls a number, cover it. One number at a time.

Phrases: Cover a number greater than.

Cover a number less than. Cover a number with ___ tens.

Cover a number equal to. Cover a number with ____ ones.

Cover a number with _____ tens and _____ones.

Cover a number in between _____ and _____.

51	43	105	10
120	50	65	90
12	111	39	77
0	27	5	82

10	34	101	72
90	45	52	75
11	109	69	81
29	100	5	0

Wednesday: Missing Numbers

Fill in the missing numbers on the piece from a hundred grid.

			35

Thursday: Number Talk

Pick a number from each circle. Add them. Decide how you will solve it and write that expression under the title.

Did I do it in my head?	Did I use a model?	Did I write down the numbers and solve it on paper?

A.

2 3 4

5 6 7 8

9 0 1

B.

2 3 4

5 6 7 8

9 0 1

Friday: Model It

There are 4 butterflies and 3 ladybugs. How many more butterflies are there than ladybugs? _____

Model it in the ten frame.

Answer:

Week 17 Teacher Notes

Monday: Missing Numbers

Students have to reason about the information given to them and then decide which child they agree with and why.

Tuesday: Vocabulary Bingo

Students listen for a strategy and then cover 1 space at a time. Whoever gets 4 in a row, across, up or down or diagonally wins. The focus of this routine is on naming different addition strategies.

Wednesday: Greater Than, Less Than, in Between

Students have to discuss the relationship of numbers. They work on using the language of comparison as well.

Thursday: Number Talk

Students discuss both addition and subtraction ways to make ten.

Friday: What's the Question? (3 Read Protocol)

Chorally read the problem 3 times before the students come up with questions.

Read the problem stem 3 times. The first time read it and ask about the context. The second time read it and talk about the numbers. The third time read it and ask what questions could be asked about the scenario. The teacher records these questions on the board. Then, the teacher gives the students time to think about the answers and discuss them.

Week 17 Activities

Monday: Missing Numbers

Who do you agree with, and why, about the answer to this problem?

3 + ___ = 7

Jen said that the answer is 10. Kelly said the answer is 4. Who is correct? How do you know?

Tuesday: Vocabulary Bingo

As your teacher calls a type of fact, cover it and say the answer. For example, the teacher says, "a doubles fact." You have to cover a doubles fact and say the answer. ONLY cover 1 type of fact at a time.

1 + 1	10 − 5	8 − 1	7 + 2	2 + 2	10 − 4	7 − 1	6 + 4
9 + 0	6 + 3	5 + 5	2 − 0	6 − 0	9 + 3	5 + 2	8 + 0
6 + 1	4 + 4	12 + 2	7 − 2	5 − 2	9 + 1	12 + 2	6 + 2
5 + 1	8 + 2	5 − 3	2 + 2	3 + 3	5 + 5	4 − 3	4 + 4

Teacher call notes: Students have to cover the fact and then say the answer.

Cover a doubles fact. Cover a plus 1 fact. (Just the next number.) Cover a count on fact (plus 1, 2, or 3).

Cover a subtract from 10 fact. (Think ten friends.) Cover a take away or add zero fact. Cover a count back fact (subtract 1, 2, or 3).

Cover a take away 1 fact. (Think the number before.) Cover a make ten fact.
Cover an add 0 fact.
Cover a subtract 0 fact.

Wednesday: Greater Than, Less Than, in Between

- Write a number greater than 15.
- Write a number less than 92.
- Write a number in between 34 and 41.

Thursday: Number Talk

Write 5 ways to make ten.

Friday: What's the Question? (3 Read Protocol)

Read the problem 3 times with your class. Then, ask questions about this story.

There were 5 apples, 3 oranges and 2 bananas. Ask 3 questions about this problem.

Week 18 Teacher Notes

Monday: True or False?

In this routine the students discuss whether or not statements are true or false.

Tuesday: What Doesn't Belong?

In this routine students have to discuss what doesn't belong. They should be able to talk about what 3 of the boxes have in common and how the other one is different. There is often more than 1 thing that can be correct.

Wednesday: Guess My Number

Students use the clues to guess the number. They can use number lines and number grids to help them.

Thursday: Number Strings

Students discuss these expressions. The focus should be on how to add 10 to a number mentally.

Friday: Problem Solving

Students have to read, solve and model a word problem.

Week 18 Activities

Monday: True or False?

Look at the boxes. Decide and discuss whether the equation is true or false.

True or False?	True or False?	Make Your Own and Share It out.
A.	B.	C.
$2 + 2 = 10 - 6$	$1 + 1 = 2 - 2$	

Tuesday: What Doesn't Belong?

Look at the options in each box. Figure out which one doesn't belong. Decide and discuss.

A.

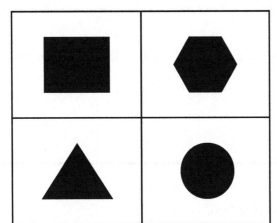

B.

$8 - 4$	$10 - 5$
$2 + 1 + 2$	$2 + 3$

Wednesday: Guess My Number

Use the clues to guess the number. Look at the hundred grid to help you figure out the number.

1	2	3	4	5	6	7	8	9	10
11	12	13	14	15	16	17	18	19	20
21	22	23	24	25	26	27	28	29	30
31	32	33	34	35	36	37	38	39	40
41	42	43	44	45	46	47	48	49	50
51	52	53	54	55	56	57	58	59	60
61	62	63	64	65	66	67	68	69	70
71	72	73	74	75	76	77	78	79	80
81	82	83	84	85	86	87	88	89	90
91	92	93	94	95	96	97	98	99	100

A.	B.
I am a 2 digit number. I am more than 12. I am less than 20. My digits add up to 9. Who am I?	The mystery number is 7. What are the clues?

Thursday: Number Strings

What are some ways to think about:

29 + 10
12 + 10
15 + 10
14 + 10

What do you notice about adding 10 to a number?

1	2	3	4	5	6	7	8	9	10
11	12	13	14	15	16	17	18	19	20
21	22	23	24	25	26	27	28	29	30
31	32	33	34	35	36	37	38	39	40
41	42	43	44	45	46	47	48	49	50
51	52	53	54	55	56	57	58	59	60
61	62	63	64	65	66	67	68	69	70
71	72	73	74	75	76	77	78	79	80
81	82	83	84	85	86	87	88	89	90
91	92	93	94	95	96	97	98	99	100

Friday: Problem Solving

At the aquarium, we saw 8 turtles. We saw 2 fewer fish than turtles. How many fish did we see?

Twenty Frame

Answer:

Week 19 Teacher Notes

Monday: How Many More to

Students have to reason about numbers. They need to know how many more to add to a given number to get the target number.

Tuesday: Vocabulary Bingo

Students listen for a strategy and then cover 1 space at a time. Whoever gets 4 in a row, across, up or down or diagonally wins. The focus in this game is on discussing subtraction strategies.

Wednesday: Number Bond It!

This is an opportunity for students to build on their work on composing and decomposing numbers.

Thursday: Number Talk

Students work on subtracting numbers. They have to discuss whether or not they did it in their head, with a drawing or on paper.

Friday: What's the Story?

Students work on telling and solving word problems using a variety of models.

Monday: How Many More to

Use the number line to figure out how many more to 20.

Start at 10 … How many more to 20?

Start at 15 … How many more to 20?

Start at 18 … How many more to 20?

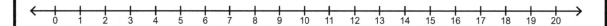

Tuesday: Vocabulary Bingo

As your teacher calls a strategy, cover one fact that matches that strategy. One space at a time.
Share the answer to the problem you covered with a neighbor.

Teacher will call out:
Taking away 1 (it's the number before)
Take away a number from itself (always zero)
Take away a number from 10 (think 10 friends)
Take away neighbor numbers (difference of 1)
Taking away 0 from a number (number stays the same)
Count back facts (count back 1, 2, or 3)

4 – 1	3 – 0	4 – 4	9 – 1	8 – 8	7 – 2	5 – 1	10 – 2
9 – 2	7 – 6	10 – 10	10 – 2	10 – 10	5 – 1	8 – 2	7 – 6
4 – 2	10 – 4	5 – 5	5 – 0	0 – 0	3 – 0	10 – 3	2 – 0
8 – 7	7 – 7	5 – 3	10 – 7	9 – 8	2 – 2	10 – 5	6 – 3

Wednesday: Number Bond It!

Show how to break apart 12 in 3 different ways!

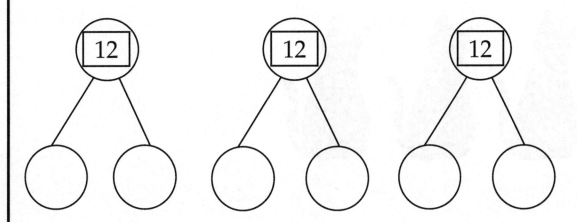

Thursday: Number Talk

Pick a number from each circle. Make a subtraction problem. Write the problem under the way you solved it.

Did I do it in my head?	Did I use a model?	Did I write down the numbers and solve it on paper?

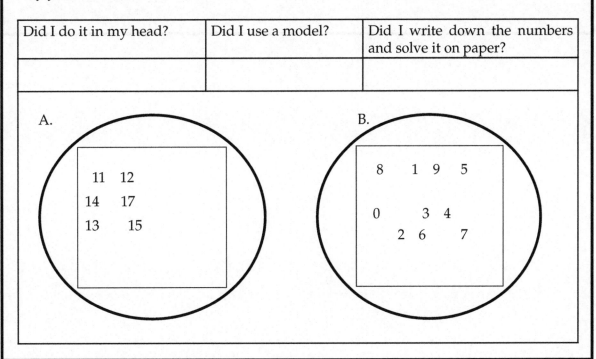

A.

11	12
14	17
13	15

B.

8 1 9 5

0   3 4

2 6   7

Friday: What's the Story?

Write a word problem where the answer is 3 cats.

Week 20 Teacher Notes

Monday: True or False?

In this routine the students discuss whether or not statements are true or false.

Tuesday: Vocabulary Brainstorm

In each thought cloud write or draw something that has to do with doubles.
For example: 2 + 2; doubles is when you add the same number together.

Wednesday: What Doesn't Belong?

In this routine students have to discuss what doesn't belong. They should be able to talk about what 3 of the boxes have in common and how the other one is different. There is often more than 1 thing that can be correct.

Thursday: Number Talk

Students are looking at patterns in expressions. They should notice that these are neighbor numbers and the difference is 1.

Friday: Problem Solving

Students work on solving word problems with a variety of models. They should recognize that this is a compare problem.

Monday: True or False?

Look at the boxes. Decide and discuss whether the equation is true or false.

	True or False?
$5 + 10 = 5 + 5 + 5$	
$12 - 8 = 8 + 4$	
$10 = 5 + 5$	
$5 - 5 = 0 - 0$	
Make Your Own!	

Tuesday: Vocabulary Brainstorm

In each thought cloud write or draw something that has to do with doubles facts

Doubles

Wednesday: What Doesn't Belong?

Look at the options in each box. Figure out which one doesn't belong. Decide and discuss.

A.

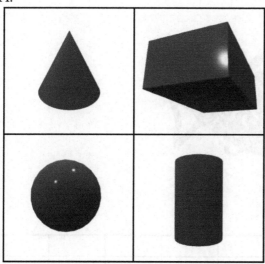

B.

2 + 2	4 − 0
10 − 7	0 + 1 + 3

Thursday: Number Talk

What are some ways to think about these problems:

5 − 4
6 − 5
7 − 6
9 − 8

What do you notice?

0 ←————————————————————→ 10

Friday: Problem Solving

In the aquarium there were 10 fish. There were 5 turtles. How many more fish than turtles were in the aquarium?

Twenty Frame

Week 21 Teacher Notes

Monday: Missing Numbers

Students are expected to reason about the missing number.

Tuesday: Vocabulary Talk

Students discuss 2D shapes. They should be able to talk about their attributes.

Wednesday: Number Bond It!

This is an opportunity for students to build on their work on composing and decomposing numbers to 14.

Thursday: Number Talk

This is an opportunity for students to discuss patterns they notice in the string.

The focus of this talk is to subtract tens.

Friday: What's the Story

Students have to tell and solve an addition or subtraction problem where the answer is 7.

Week 21 Activities

Monday: Missing Numbers

3 – _____ = 0

1 – _____ = 0

10 – _____ = 0

How are these problems alike?

Think about it.

1. Share your thinking with a friend. Defend your answer.
2. Share your thinking with the group.

Tuesday: Vocabulary Talk

Name and discuss 2D shapes. Why are they 2D?

Wednesday: Number Bond It!

Show how to break apart 14 in 3 different ways!

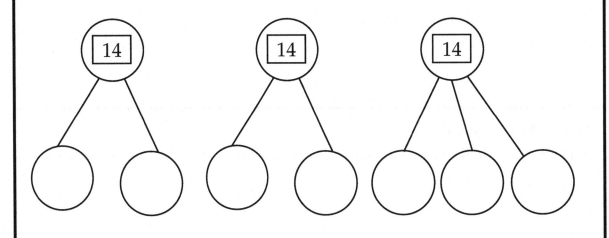

Thursday: Number Talk

Pick a number from each circle. Make a subtraction problem. Write the problem under the way you solved it.

Did I do it in my head?	Did I use a model?	Did I write down the numbers and solve it on paper?

A.

10 20 30 40

50 60 70 80 90

B.

10

Friday: What's the Story?

The answer is 7 dogs. What is the story?

Story:

Model:

Equation:

Answer:

Week 22 Teacher Notes

Monday: True or False?

In this routine the students discuss whether or not statements are true or false.

Tuesday: Frayer Model

Students have to discuss the word. Fill in the boxes to describe and give examples of the word.

Wednesday: Number Line It!

Students have to discuss how to order and plot the numbers on the number line from least to greatest.

Thursday: Number Strings

Students are looking at patterns in expressions.

The focus of this discussion is on bridging 10.

Friday: What's the Question? (3 Read Protocol)

Chorally read the problem 3 times before the students come up with questions.

The first time read it and ask about the context. The second time read it and talk about the numbers. The third time read it and ask what questions could be asked about the scenario. The teacher records these questions on the board. Then, the teacher gives the students time to think about the answers and discuss them.

Week 22 Activities

Monday: True or False?

Look at the boxes. Decide and discuss whether the equation is true or false.

Mark said that $4 + 4 = 1 + 3 + 4$.

Can that be true?

Tuesday: Frayer Model

Discuss the word. Fill in the boxes to describe and give examples of the word.

Difference

Definition	Examples
Give a Picture Example	Non-examples

Wednesday: Number Line It!

Put the numbers from least to greatest on it. Space them out as accurately as possible.

118, 50, 2, 90

0 ⟵――――――――――――――――――――――――――→ 120

Thursday: Number Strings

Talk about how bridging through 10 helps us solve these:

9 + 2
9 + 3
9 + 4
9 + 5
9 + 6
9 + 8
9 + 9

0   20

Friday: What's the Question? (3 Read Protocol)

Read the problem 3 times with your class.

Think of at least 2 questions you could ask about this story. Write them down. Discuss with your classmates.

Mary has 3 purple rings, 2 pink rings and 4 yellow rings.

1.

2.

Week 23 Teacher Notes

Monday: Magic Square

Students have to fill in the missing number so that it makes 15 up, down, across and diagonally. They have to use each of the digits 1 through 9 once.

Tuesday: Frayer Model

Students have to discuss the word. Fill in the boxes to describe and give examples of the word.

Wednesday: Number of the Day

Students have to fill in the boxes to represent the number 18. Have the students do it on their own, discuss with a partner and then debrief the whole class.

Thursday: Number Strings

The focus of this conversation is on subtracting from 10.

Friday: Problem Solving

In this activity students are working on modeling a part-part whole problem.

Monday: Magic Square

The sum is 15!

Look at the square. You have to fill in the missing number so that it make 15 up, down, across and diagonally. Use each of the digits 1 through 9 once.

8		6
	5	7
4		

Tuesday: Frayer Model

Discuss the word. Fill in the boxes to describe and give examples of the word.

Compare

Definition	Examples
Give a Picture Example	**Non-examples**

Wednesday: Number of the Day

Look at the number and fill in the boxes to match the number.

18

How many tens? _____ How many ones? _____	Base 10 sketch
Model on the twenty frame 	___ + ___ = 18 ___ – ___ = 18

Thursday: Number Strings

What are some strategies to solve facts where we take away from 10?

10 – 7
10 – 6
10 – 5
10 – 4
10 – 3

How can the tens friend strategy help us?

Friday: Problem Solving

In the aquarium there are 8 animals. There were 5 fish. The rest were turtles. How many animals were turtles?

Model it on the twenty frame.

Answer:

Week 24 Teacher Notes

Monday: Reasoning Matrices

Students have to reason about the information given to them and then decide which child matches the description.

Tuesday: Vocabulary Quick-Write

Students have a minute to write everything they know about addition. They then give it to a friend to read and add something to their paper. They get their paper back and write for another 30 seconds. Then they discuss what they have done.

Wednesday: Number Line It!

Students have to discuss how to order and plot the numbers on the number line from least to greatest.

Thursday: Number Talk

Students work on subtracting multiples of ten from multiples of ten within 100. They have to discuss whether or not they did it in their head, with a drawing or on paper.

Friday: Model It

Students solve a part-part whole problem.

Monday: Reasoning Matrices

Sue likes to play on the slide. Lucy likes to play on the playground set where she can do a lot of things at once. Marvin likes to climb bars. Carl will play on anything.

Sue				
Carl				
Lucy				
Marvin				

Tuesday: Vocabulary Quick-Write

You have 1 minute to write everything you know about addition.

Go!

Share your paper with a friend. Your friend adds 1 thing to your paper.

Switch back and add 1 more thing to your paper.

Wednesday: Number Line It!

Think about the order of numbers. Line them up from least to greatest on the number line as accurately as possible.

50, 10, 100, 70, 90, 30

0 ←――――――――――――――――――――――――――→ 120

Thursday: Number Talk

Pick a number from each circle. Subtract them. Decide how you will solve it and write that expression under the title.

Did I do it in my head?	Did I use a model?	Did I write down the numbers and solve it on paper?

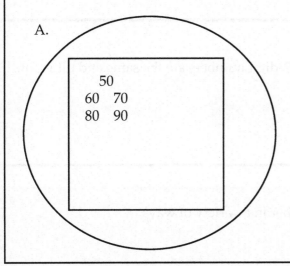

A.

50
60   70
80   90

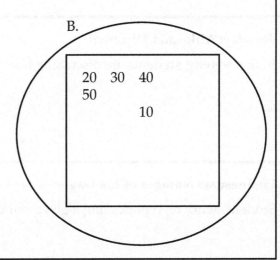

B.

20   30   40
50
10

Friday: Model It

There were 6 butterflies and some ladybugs. There were 14 insects altogether. How many ladybugs were there?

Draw it in the twenty frame.

Answer:

Week 25 Teacher Notes

Monday: What Doesn't Belong?

In this activity, students have to look at equations and decide which one is not like the others.

Tuesday: Alike and Different

In this activity, students are discussing how 2-digit numbers are the same and different.

Wednesday: Number of the Day

Students work on representing a given number in a variety of ways.

Thursday: Number Strings

The focus of this discussion should be on bridging 10. Students can talk about counting up or counting back (using 10 as a bridge).

Students can also talk about taking away 10 and then adding back 1. For example, $12 - 9$ would be 2 plus 1 more which makes 3.

Friday: Make Your Own Problem

Students make their own problem by filling in numbers. They have to then model it and write a number sentence and share their thinking with their math partner.

Week 25 Activities

Monday: What Doesn't Belong?

Look at the options in each box. Figure out which one doesn't belong. Decide and Discuss.

A.

60 – 30	20 + 10
30 – 30	40 – 10

B.

3 + 7 + 5	8 + 8
16 – 1	20 – 5

Tuesday: Alike and Different

Look at the numbers and decide and discuss how they are alike and how they are different.

16 and 61

Alike	Different

Word bank: less than, more than, greater than, same as, ones, tens digits.

Wednesday: Number of the Day

Look at the number and fill in the boxes to match the number.

20

How many tens? _ How many ones? _	10 more	10 less
Tens Ones	_____ + _____ = 20	Base 10 sketch

Thursday: Number Strings

14 – 9

13 – 9

12 – 9

11 – 9

How does the bridge through ten strategy help us subtract 9 from a number?

0   20

Friday: Make Your Own Problem

Write and solve your own word problem. Use a number between 0 and 10 in each space.

The store had _____ rings. It got _____ more. How many does it have now?

Model it.

Number sentence (equation): _____
Answer:

Monday: Always, Sometimes, Never

Students have to listen to the statement and then discuss and decide if this statement is always, sometime or never true!

Tuesday: Frayer Model

Students have to discuss the word. Fill in the boxes to describe and give examples of the word.

Wednesday: Compose It!

Students have to use 2 different crayons (colors) to show 4 ways to make the number 6 on the models below. They should do it, explain their thinking to a partner and then discuss their ways with the class.

Thursday: Number Strings

Students are looking at patterns in expressions.

The focus in this conversation is bridging 10 when subtracting 8. Students should talk about different ways to subtract 8 including either counting up or counting back with 10 as a bridge.

Friday: What's the Story?

Students have to match the equation with the story.

Week 26 Activities

Monday: Always, Sometimes, Never

Discuss and decide if this statement is always, sometime or never true!

When you add two numbers, the sum is greater than each of the two addends.	Prove it!

Tuesday: Frayer Model

Cube

Definition	Examples
Give a Picture Example	Non-examples

Wednesday: Compose It!

Use the models to show 4 different ways to make 8. Share your thinking with a partner. Be ready to discuss with the class.

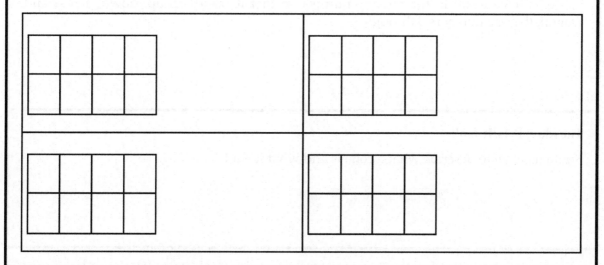

Thursday: Number Strings

What are some ways to solve:

11 – 8
12 – 8
13 – 8
14 – 8
15 – 8

How does bridging through 10 help us to subtract 8 from a number?

0   20

Friday: What's the Story?

Look at the equation. Match the equation with the story:

5 – ? = 1

Problem A	Problem B
Kelly had 5 marbles. She got 1 more. How many does she have now?	Kelly had 5 marbles. She gave some away and now she has 1. How many did she give away?

Monday: Magic Square

Students have to fill in the missing number so that it makes 15 up, down, across and diagonally. Use numbers 0 through 9.

Tuesday: It Is/It Isn't

Students have to describe what a cone is and what it isn't.

Wednesday: Greater Than, Less Than, in Between

Students have to discuss the relationship of numbers. They work on using the language of comparison as well. Answers vary.

Thursday: Number Strings

Students are looking at patterns in expressions. They have to discuss what it means to be a half fact and name 2 that are not listed.

Friday: What's the Story?

Students need to make up a story to match the model. Answers vary. For example, Sue had 10 marbles and she gave 2 away. How many does she have now?

Week 27 Activities

Monday: Magic Square

The sum is 15.

Look at the squares. You have to fill in the missing number so that it makes 15 up, down, across and diagonally. Use digits 0 through 9 once.

2		6
	5	
	3	

Tuesday: It Is/It Isn't

Describe what the word is and what it isn't.

Cone

It Is	It Isn't

Wednesday: Greater Than, Less Than, in Between

99   108   120

Name a number less than 99	Name a number greater than 108	Name a number less than 120
Name a number greater than 99	Name a number in between 99 and 108	Name a number in between 108 and 120

Thursday: Number Strings

Discuss what these expressions have in common.

4 – 2
6 – 3
8 – 4
10 – 5

Friday: What's the Story?

Look at the model. Tell a story about it.

Story:

Equation:

Answer:

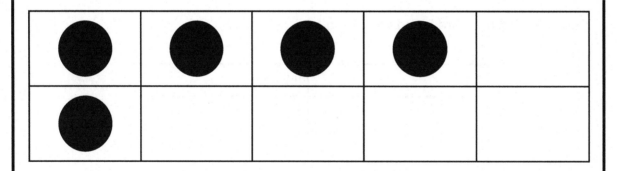

Week 28 Teacher Notes

Monday: Missing Numbers

Students have to fill in the missing numbers on the hundred grid chart.

Tuesday: Vocabulary Fill-in

Students have to use the words in the word bank to fill in the blanks.

Wednesday: Legs and Feet

Students have to reason about how many legs and feet there are given the number of animals shown.

Thursday: Number Talk

Students should discuss different ways to solve this problem.

Friday: What's the Problem?

Students have to reason and decide which is the comparison problem. They should be able to justify why it is a comparison problem and model it.

Monday: Missing Numbers

Fill in the missing numbers on the piece from a hundred grid.

				55		

Tuesday: Vocabulary Fill-in

Fill in using the words in the word bank to fill in the blanks below.

Word bank: addend, doubles, difference, sum, equal.

When you add a number to itself it is a _____ fact.

_____ means "the same as".

The answer to an addition problem is the _____.

The answer to a subtraction problem is the _____.

The _____ is one of the numbers you add in an addition problem.

Wednesday: Legs and Feet

There is a turtle and a duck.

A. How many legs? 	B. If there are 12 legs and there has to be a duck and a turtle, how many animals and what type are there? C. What if there were 14 legs?

Thursday: Number Talk

What are some ways to subtract 8 from 12?

Friday: What's the Problem?

Circle the compare problem. How do you know it is a compare problem? Are you looking for the bigger part, the smaller part or the difference?

Luke has 5 red marbles and 5 green ones. How many does he have altogether?

Maria has 4 marbles. Her sister has 2 more than she does. How many does her sister have?

Jamal had 5 marbles. His sister gave him 1 more. How many does he have now?

Monday: Magic Square

Students have to fill in the missing number so that it makes 15 up, down, across and diagonally. Use numbers 0 through 9.

Tuesday: Frayer Model

Students have to discuss the word. Fill in the boxes to describe and give examples of the word.

Wednesday: Number of the Day

Students have to fill in the boxes to represent the number 10. Have the students do it on their own, discuss with a partner and then debrief with the whole class.

Thursday: Number Talk

Students work on subtracting numbers from 10.

Friday: Model It

Students have to model the problem and write the equation.

Monday: Magic Square

The sum is 15.

Fill in the missing number by making 15 up, down, across and diagonally.

6	1	
	5	

Tuesday: Frayer Model

Discuss the word. Fill in the boxes to describe and give examples of the word.

Sphere

Definition	Examples
Give a Picture Example	Non-examples

Wednesday: Number of the Day

Look at the number and fill in the boxes to match the number.

57

Base 10 sketch	57 is greater than_____ 57 is less than _____
Tens _____ Ones _____	$57 + 10 =$ $57 - 10 =$

Thursday: Number Talk

Pick a number from each circle. Subtract them. Decide how you will solve it and write that expression under the title.

Did I do it in my head?	Did I use a model?	Did I write down the numbers and solve it on paper?

A.

7 8 9 10

B.

1 2 3
4 5 6

0   10

Friday: Model It

In the aquarium there were 4 fish. Then some more swam up. Now there are 10 fish. How many swam up?

Equation:

Sketch It:

Model it on the ten frame.

Week 30 Teacher Notes

Monday: 3 Truths and a Fib

Students have to discuss and decide which statements are true and which ones are false. They have to explain their thinking to their neighbor and then the group.

Tuesday: Vocabulary Brainstorm

In each thought cloud, students have to write or draw something that has to do with geometry.

Wednesday: Number Line It!

Students have to discuss how to order and plot the numbers on the number line from least to greatest.

Thursday: Number String

Students are looking at patterns in expressions. They are discussing half facts.

Friday: What's the Question? (3 Read Protocol)

Chorally read the problem 3 times before the students come up with questions.

The first time read it and ask about the context. The second time read it and talk about the numbers. The third time read it and ask what questions could be asked about the scenario. The teacher records these questions on the board. Then give the students time to think about the answers and discuss them.

Week 30 Activities

Monday: 3 Truths and a Fib

Discuss and decide. Which one is false? Why? Explain to your neighbor and then the group.

31 < 56	17 > 10
4 = 2 + 2	10 < 7

Tuesday: Vocabulary Brainstorm

In each thought cloud write or draw something that has to do with geometry.

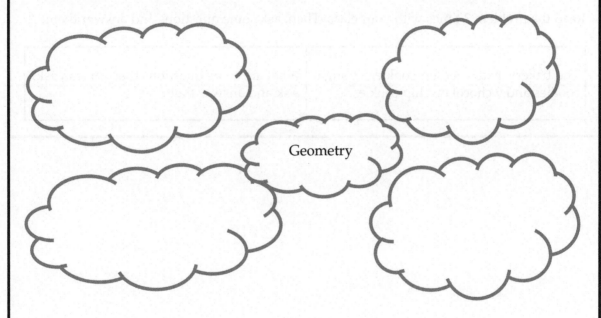

Geometry

Wednesday: Number Line It!

Think about the order of numbers. Line them up from least to greatest on the number line as accurately as possible.

25, 7, 120, 50

0

Thursday: Number Strings

What are some ways to think about these types of problems?

$2 - 1$
$4 - 2$
$6 - 3$
$8 - 4$
$10 - 5$

What types of facts are these? What addition facts can help us solve these quickly?

Friday: What's the Question? (3 Read Protocol)

Read the problem 3 times with your class. Then, ask some questions and answer them.

The bakery had 2 lemon cookies, 4 sugar cookies and 9 chocolate chip cookies.	What are some questions that you can ask? Ask and answer them.

Monday: 2 Arguments

Students have to discuss and decide who is correct. They need to defend their thinking with a partner. This is an opportunity to discuss the meaning of the equal sign.

Tuesday: Vocabulary Match

Students have to match the word with the correct definition.

Wednesday: Alike and Different

The focus is on place value vocabulary. Students should use the word bank to scaffold their conversation.

Thursday: Number Talk

The focus of this conversation should be subtracting 7 from a number, using a variety of strategies including bridging 10 by counting up or back.

Friday: What's the Story?

In this problem, students are making up word problems where the answer is 7 dogs. Discuss the answer with the students and then give them think time on their own and then with a partner. Then, have the class come back together and share their ideas with the whole class and discuss the different stories. The teacher should try to get both addition and subtraction stories.

Monday: 2 Arguments

Discuss and decide who is correct.

8 + ____ = 10

John said the answer was 18.

Maria said the answer was 2.

Who do you agree with?

Why?

Tuesday: Vocabulary Match

Match the word with the correct definition by drawing lines from the definition to the correct example.

Hundreds
place

Hexagon   Answer to an
                    addition problem

Tens place   18

Ones place   14

Sum   160

Wednesday: Alike and Different

Discuss how these numbers are alike and different. Use the word bank to get started.

120 and 12

Alike	Different

Word bank: single digit, double digit, triple digit, ones place, tens place, hundreds place, greater than, less than, equal to, same as.

Thursday: Number Talk

What are some ways to solve these problems:

$11 - 7$
$15 - 7$
$13 - 7$
$12 - 7$
$16 - 7$

0 ⟵————————————————————⟶ 20

Friday: What's the Story?

Tell a math story about these 7 dogs.

Story:

Equation:

Week 32 Teacher Notes

Monday: Graphs

Students have to read the information and then make a graph based on that information and ask questions about the information.

Tuesday: Vocabulary Match

Students have to match the word with the correct definition.

Wednesday: Convince Me!

Students have to discuss whether or not the equation is true or false. They must defend their thinking.

Thursday: Number Talk

In this routine, students get to make their own subtraction problems. After they solve them, they will discuss their strategies.

Friday: Equation Match

Students have to reason about the problem and match the equation with the story.

Monday: Graphs

Read the information in the table and use to ask 3 questions.

Our Favorite Animals

dogs	10
cats	8
birds	5
fish	2
other	3

Tuesday: Vocabulary Match

Match the word with the correct definition by drawing lines between the definition and the descriptions.

Make Ten Fact   A problem where you take away half of a number from its double

Doubles Fact   Pairs of numbers that make ten

Length   How long something is

Greater Than   An addition problem when you add a number to itself

Half Fact   Bigger, more or larger than

Wednesday: Convince Me!

Prove it with numbers, words and/or pictures!

$2 + 8 = 20 - 10$

Thursday: Number Talk

Pick a number from each circle. Decide how you are going to solve subtracting one number from the other. Write the problem under the way you solved it. For example, $18 - 9$. I can do that in my head because I know $9 + 9$ is 18.

Did I do it in my head?	Did I use a model?	Did I write down the numbers and solve it on paper?

A.

```
10  12  14  16

   18  20

13  15  17  19  11
```

B.

```
10  9  8  7
  6  5  4

   2  1
```

Friday: Equation Match

$10 + \underline{\quad} = 12$

Which problem matches the equation?

1. The bakery had 10 cookies. They made some more. Now they have 12 cookies. How many did they make?

2. The bakery had some cookies. They made some more. Now they have 12. How many did they make?

3. The bakery made 10 cookies and then they made 12 more. How many do they have now?

Week 33 Teacher Notes

Monday: What Doesn't Belong?

Students have to choose which clock does not belong. They need to discuss why.

Tuesday: Vocabulary Match

Students have to match the word with the definition.

Wednesday: Number of the Day

Students have to fill in the boxes to represent the number 100. Have the students do it on their own, discuss with a partner and then debrief with the whole class.

Thursday: Number Strings

In this number string students are discussing how to take away 7 from a number. They should be discussing counting back and counting up and bridging 10.

Friday: Model It

In this routine, students are looking at the both addends unknown problem type. They should draw pictures to match the table.

Monday: What Doesn't Belong?

Look at the options in each box. Figure out which one doesn't belong. Decide and discuss.

Tuesday: Vocabulary Match

Match the word with the correct definition.

Half Past 2		
Noon		
1:30		
3:00		

Wednesday: Number of the Day

Look at the number and fill in the boxes to match the number.

100

Number line it!	Write the number
⬅————————➡	
Base 10 sketch	100 is greater than _____ 100 is less than _____ 100 is the same as _____

Thursday: Number Strings

What are some strategies for subtracting 7?

12 – 7
15 – 7
16 – 7
11 – 7
13 – 7

⬅————————————————————➡

0   20

Friday: Model It

Grandma made 2 sandwiches that were the same size. She cut Joel's in 2 parts and Maria's in 4 parts.

Joel said that Maria got more than he did. Grandma said they got the same amount. Who do you agree with? Why?

Maria	Joel

I agree with _____ because _____

Week 34 Teacher Notes

Monday: Reasoning Matrices

Students have to reason about the information given to them and then decide which child matches the description.

Tuesday: Vocabulary Match

Students have to match the word with the correct definition.

Wednesday: Convince Me!

Students have to convince each other that this is a triangle by discussing its attributes.

Thursday: Number Talk

Students have to look at the pattern in the expressions and discuss what happens when you add multiples of tens to multiples of tens.

Friday: Picture That!

Students use the picture prompts to tell and represent a story where the answer is 5.

Monday: Reasoning Matrices

Sue likes animals that you can ride. Lucy likes to play in the mud. Marvin loves milk. Carl loves wooly hats. What could be these children's favorite farm animals be?

Sue				
Carl				
Lucy				
Marvin				

Tuesday: Vocabulary Match

Match the word with the correct definition.

Thirds		
Equal		The Same as
Halves		
Fourths		

Convince Me!

Convince me that this is a triangle.

Thursday: Number Talk

Pick a number from each circle Decide how you are going to solve the addition of the two numbers. Write the problem under the way you solved it.

Did I do it in my head?	Did I use a model?	Did I write down the numbers and solve it on paper?

20   30   40
50   60   70   80
90

10   20   30
40
50

Friday: Picture That!

Tell a word problem about birds, where the answer is 5.

Story:

Model:

Equation:

Week 35 Teacher Notes

Monday: True or False?

In this routine the students discuss whether or not the figure is a hexagon. They should center their discussion around the attributes of hexagons.

Tuesday: Vocabulary Tic Tac Toe

Students have to discuss the words with their partner. They have to draw or write or explain their thinking before they put the x or o. Whoever gets 3 in a row first wins.

Wednesday: Number Bond It!

In this routine, students will discuss the number 19 and how to represent it in a variety of ways.

Thursday: Number Talk

Students discuss subtracting from 20.

Friday: Make Your Own Problem

In this routine, students get to pick their own numbers to make a problem and then solve it.

Monday: True or False?

Look at the shape. Decide and discuss whether the statement is true or false.

This is a hexagon.

1. Think about it.
2. Share your thinking with a friend. Defend your answer.
3. Share your thinking with the group.
4. Draw another type of hexagon.

Tuesday: Vocabulary Tic Tac Toe

Play this game with your math partner. Play rock, paper and scissors to see who starts. Take turns, choosing a problem. Explain to your partner how you got the answer. Whoever gets 3 in a row first wins. At the end, discuss your strategies with the whole class.

A.

2 + 2	7 + 3	3 + 4
0 + 1	6 + 2	4 + 1
9 + 1	5 + 3	8 + 2

B.

2 − 2	10 − 7	7 − 5
3 − 0	9 − 8	4 − 2
6 − 1	8 − 6	5 − 4

Wednesday: Number Bond It!

Show how to break apart 19 in 3 different ways!

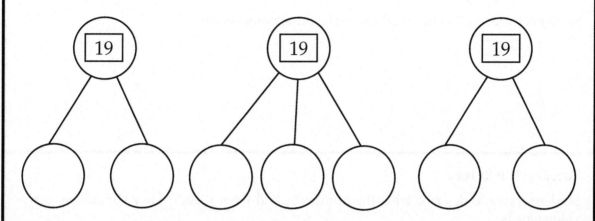

Thursday: Number Talk

What are some ways to solve 20 – 5?

Friday: Make Your Own Problem

Use digits between 0 and 9.

Sue had _____marbles. She got _____ more for her birthday. How many does she have now?

Model it.

Number sentence (equation): _____.

Week 36 Teacher Notes

Monday: Missing Numbers

Students have to fill in the blanks to make the statements true.

Tuesday: It Is/It Isn't

Students have to describe what the number is and what it isn't. They should use place value words.

Wednesday: Greater Than, Less Than, in Between

Students have to discuss the relationship of numbers. They work on using the language of comparison as well.

Thursday: Number Talk

Students will look at ways to add a single digit and a double digit number. The discussion should focus on bridging the next ten.

Friday: Equation Match

Students have to match the equation with the story.

Monday: Missing Numbers

Fill in the blanks below to make true statements.

Explain what you did to your neighbor.

Be ready to discuss your thinking with the whole class.

_____ < _____

_____ > _____

_____ = _____

Tuesday: It Is/It Isn't

Describe what the number is and what it isn't.

50

It Is	It Isn't

Word bank: less than, more than, greater than, same as, equal to, digit, odd, even.

Wednesday: Greater Than, Less Than, in Between

82 100 110

Name a number greater than 82.	Name a number less than 110.	Name a number less than 100.
Name a number greater than 110.	Name a number in between 82 and 110.	Name a number in between 100 and 110.

Thursday: Number Talk

What is a way to add these numbers:

74 + 8
34 + 9
23 + 7
56 + 9

What are some strategies to use when adding these numbers?

Friday: Equation Match

Which equation matches the story and why?

Jan had 10 marbles. She got some more. Now she has 20. How many did she get?

A. 10 + ? = 20
B. ? + 10 = 20
C. 20 + 10 = ?
D. Equation is not here.

Week 37 Teacher Notes

Monday: How Many More to

Students have to reason about numbers. They need to know how many more to a given number.

Tuesday: Vocabulary Bingo

Students listen for a strategy and then cover 1 space at a time. Whoever gets 4 in a row, across, up or down or diagonally wins.

Wednesday: Guess My Number

Students use the clues to guess the number. They can use number lines and number grids to help them.

Thursday: Number Talk

Students should discuss adding doubles plus 1 facts. They should talk about how doubles can be a helper fact.

Friday: What's the Story?

In this routine, the students are given a number line model and asked to tell a story about the numbers that are modeled on it.

Monday: How Many More to

Use the number line to help scaffold your thinking.

Start at 10 … How many more to 20?

Start at 11 … How many more to 20?

Start at 15 … How many more to 20?

1	2	3	4	5	6	7	87	9	10	11	12	13	14	15	16	17	18	19	20

Tuesday: Vocabulary Bingo

The teacher calls out different addition and subtraction strategies.

Students cover 1 space that they could use that strategy to solve. Only cover 1 fact at a time. Whoever gets all in the row across, down, diagonally or all 4 corners wins.

9 – 1	3 – 0	4 + 4	9 – 9
9 – 2	7 + 3	10 – 9	10 - 2
8 – 3	10 + 0	10 – 5	5 – 0
8 – 7	7 – 7	5 – 3	10 – 7

9 – 9	5 - 2	7 + 2	10 – 5
7 – 7	5 – 1	8 – 2	6 - 3
0 – 0	10 – 5	9 – 8	4 + 4
6 – 5	8 + 0	7 + 3	6 – 3

Wednesday: Guess My Number

Use the clues to guess the number. Look at the hundred grid to help you figure out the number.

A.	B.
I am a 3 digit number.	I am a 2 digit number.
I am greater than 50 + 50.	I am less than 70 - 50.
I am less than 120.	I am greater than 8 + 8.
I have a 0 in the ones place.	I am an even number.
Who am I?	Who am I?

Thursday: Number Talk

How could you solve ...?

2 + 3
3 + 4
4 + 5
5 + 6

What helper fact could you use?

Friday: What's the Story?

John has 8 marbles. His brother has 2 more than he does. How many does his brother have?

Model in the twenty frame.

John									
Brother									

Monday: Graphs

Students have to read the frequency table, make a bar diagram and ask questions about the data.

Tuesday: Vocabulary Tic Tac Toe

Students have to discuss the words with their partner. They have to draw or write or explain their thinking before they put the x or o. Whoever gets 3 in a row first wins.

Answers vary.

Wednesday: Missing Numbers

Students have to fill in the blanks to make the statement true.

Thursday: Number Talk

In this number talk, students will make up their own problems. They will write 5 numbers into each circle and decide whether they want to add or subtract. They will then solve their problem and discuss how they did it.

Friday: Problem Solving

Students will use the illustration to tell and solve a word problem.

Monday: Graphs

Use the information below to answer the questions.

Our Favorite Animals

Animals	Votes
Dogs	8
Cats	3
Birds	4
Fish	2
Other	3

Make a bar graph with the data.

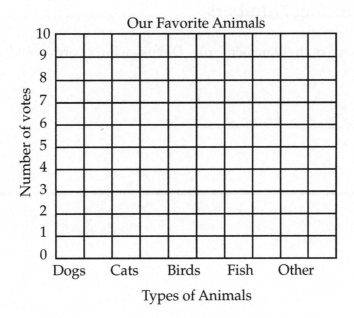

Our Favorite Animals

Ask 3 questions about this graph.

Tuesday: Vocabulary Tic Tac Toe

Write down or draw 5 different math words that you learned this year.

Wednesday: Missing Numbers

Fill in the blanks to make the statement true. Discuss with a partner and then with the whole class.

_____ + _____ > _____ + _____

Thursday: Number Talk

Pick a number from each circle Then, decide how you are going to solve it. Write the problem under the way you solved it. I can do that in my head because it is a ten friend.

Did I do it in my head?	Did I use a model?	Did I write down the numbers and solve it on paper?

29 33 47 59
65   77   86

5   6   7
  8   9

Friday: Problem Solving

Tell a story about this picture. It can be a join, take away, part-part whole or compare story.

Story:

Model:

Equation:

Monday: Graphs

Students have to read the information in the chart. Use it to make a graph and then ask questions about the graph.

Tuesday: Vocabulary Tic Tac Toe

Students have to discuss the word with their partner. They have to draw or write or explain their thinking before they put the x or o. Whoever gets 3 in a row first wins.

Answers vary.

Wednesday: Number Line It!

Students have to draw a number line and then write 5 numbers between 0 and 120 from least to greatest on the number line.

Thursday: Number Talk

Students have to write in 4 numbers in each circle. They pick a number from each circle. and then make a subtraction problem. They then decide how to solve it. They must write the problem under the way they solved it.

Friday: Model It

Students have to use the pictures to model the story.

Monday: Graphs

Use the information in the table to do the parts below.

Our Favorite Pies

Flavors	Votes
Strawberry	7
Lemon	4
Apple	5
Other	3

Make a picture graph:

Strawberry	
Lemon	
Apple	
Other	

Key 1 🙂 = 1 vote

Ask 3 questions about this graph.

Tuesday: Vocabulary Tic Tac Toe

Play this game with your math partner. For each word that you pick, draw a picture or write a definition on the side. Then put an x or an o. Whoever gets 3 in a row first wins.

tens	hundreds	+
4 + 1 = 5	=	–
ones	<	>

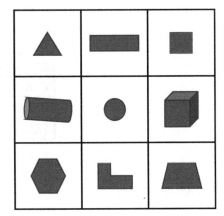

Wednesday: Number Line It!

Draw a number line. Write 5 numbers between 0 to 120 from least to greatest on the number line.

Thursday: Number Talk

A. Add 2 numbers that almost make 14.

B. Subtract 2 numbers that almost make 10.

Friday: Model It

Maria ate $\frac{1}{3}$ of her sandwich. Joel ate $\frac{1}{2}$ of his sandwich. Who ate more?
Use the pictures to model your thinking.

Maria	Joel

Monday: Reasoning Matrices

In this activity, students have to read the clues to figure out which child likes which animal.

Tuesday: Vocabulary Tic Tac Toe

Students have to discuss the words with their partner. They have to draw or write or explain their thinking before they put the x or o. Whoever gets 3 in a row first wins.

Wednesday: Magic Square

Students solve for the missing number in a magic square puzzle. They are given a number of the magic square that must work in all directions and then they have to figure out what to put in the space to make that number.

Thursday: Number Talk

In this activity students get to choose their own numbers and make their own problems. Teacher asks students how they solved it. Answers will vary. Some students will do it in their head, others will do it on a model and some will write it down on paper.

Friday: What's the Question?

Students have to read the problem and then model it using the figures provided. They need to then explain their thinking.

Monday: Reasoning Matrices

Read the clues and figure out which child likes which animal. Sue loves animals with tusks. Carl loves animals with stripes. Lucy loves animals that are tall. Marvin loves animals that live in trees.

Sue				
Carl				
Lucy				
Marvin				

Tuesday: Vocabulary Tic Tac Toe

Play this game with your math partner. For each picture that you pick, explain it to your partner. Then, put an x or an o. Whoever gets 3 in a row first wins.

Fourths	Halves	Thirds
☐☐☐☐	☐☐	☐☐☐
Fraction	**Quarter**	**Whole**
☐☐☐☐ ☐☐	■☐☐☐	☐
One-fourth	**A third of**	**Half**
■☐☐☐	■☐☐	■☐

Wednesday: Magic Square

The magic number should make 18 up, down, across, and diagonally.

3		5
7		9

Thursday: Number Talk

Pick a number from each circle. Make a problem. Decide how you will solve it and write that expression under the title. You can do an addition or subtraction problem.

Did I do it in my head?	Did I use a model?	Did I write down the numbers and solve it on paper?

A.

```
  1    2    3
   4   5   0

 6 7  8   9 10
```

B.

```
  1    2    3
   4   5    0

  6 7  8   9 10
```

Friday: What's the Question?

Read the problem 3 times with your class. Then ask and answer questions about the story.

The bakery had 2 lemon cookies and 5 sugar cookies.	What are some questions that you can ask?

Answer Key

Week 1

Monday: What Doesn't Belong?

In this routine students have to discuss what 3 belong.

A. 42.

B. 7 – 5.

Tuesday: Alike and Different

Students should be able to discuss how the shapes are alike with sides that are closed, how they have points (vertices) and how the sides are straight. We want to focus on the attributes of the shapes.

For example, they both are polygons. They both have straight sides. The triangle only has 3 sides. The square has 4 sides.

Wednesday: Number Bond It!

Composing and decomposing numbers to 10 is a kindergarten skill. Some students have not yet become proficient with this skill. This should be an activity that you do often with your students. They should have to discuss different ways to compose and decompose numbers.

For example, 5 + 5, 4 + 6, or 3 + 7.

Thursday: Number Talk

Students should be talking about what happens when you add 1 to a number. Students should talk about how it is just the next number.

Friday: What's the Story?

Students should discuss the picture and tell a story. They could tell a part-part whole story. There are 4 cats and 1 dog. How many animals are there altogether?

Week 2

Monday: True or False?

Students discuss whether the problems are true or false. They should have to think about it and prove it with a model.

A. False.
B. True.
C. False.
D. True.

Tuesday: It Is/It Isn't

16

It Is	It Isn't
2 digit number it has a ten and a six it is a teen number it is greater than 5 it is less than 20	1 digit number Less than 10 More than 20

Wednesday: Number Line It!

Students discuss the correct order of the numbers.

2, 3, 5, 7, 9

Thursday: Number Talk

Answers vary. Students have to pick numbers and discuss the addition facts with their neighbors. They should prove they are correct. For example, students might say 5 and 5 are ten and model it with their fingers.

Friday: Model It

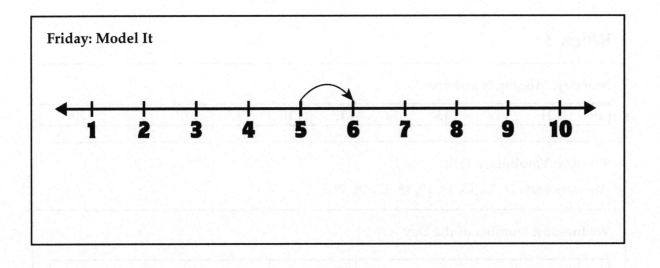

Week 3

Monday: Missing Numbers

10	11	12	13	**14**	15	16	17	18	19	20

Tuesday: Vocabulary Talk

Answers vary. 11, 12, 13, 14, 15, 16, 17, 18, 19.

Wednesday: Number of the Day

Number word	Ten frame
Ten	O O O O O O O O O O

Write the number.

10

Thursday: Number Talk

Answers vary. For example 3 + 4 or 8 – 1.

Friday: What's the Story?

Answers vary. They should draw a picture and model it in the ten frame.

Week 4

Monday: 2 Arguments

Students should talk about how the answer is 0 so they agree with John. They should have to prove how they know that it is 0 with various models.

Tuesday: It Is/It Isn't

Square

It Is	It Isn't
A shape Has 4 sides A polygon Sides are straight Sides are closed 4 vertices (corners)	A circle It doesn't have curved sides It doesn't have open sides It doesn't have 3 vertices

Wednesday: How Many More to 10

Start at 0 – 10 more
Start at 1 – 9 more
Start at 3 – 7 more
Start at 7 – 3 more
Start at 4 – 6 more
Start at 9 – 1 more
Start at 2 – 8 more

Thursday: Number Talk

The focus should be on subtracting 1 from a number. Students should realize and discuss that it is just the number before.

$5 - 1 = 4$
$4 - 1 = 3$
$3 - 1 = 2$
$7 - 1 = 6$

What happens when you subtract 1 from a number?

Friday: Picture That!

Have students tell a story about this picture

For example: There were 5 oranges and 4 bananas. How many fruits are there? $5 + 4 = 9$

Week 5

Monday: True or False?

Answers vary. Students have to populate the Bingo board with the numbers. Play Bingo. The teacher calls out the number or shows the quantity and the students mark it. Whoever gets 3 in a row first wins.

A. False.
B. True.
C. True.
D. False.

Tuesday: Vocabulary Match

This routine gives students an opportunity to discuss the shapes.

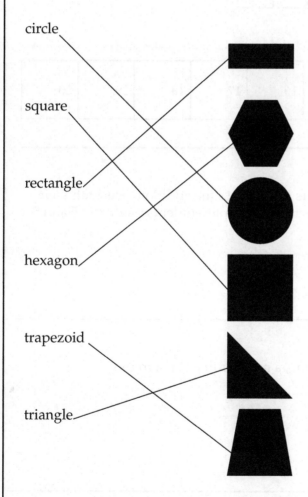

circle

square

rectangle

hexagon

trapezoid

triangle

*Be sure to talk about how a square is a special kind of rectangle.

Wednesday: Number of the Day

14

Write the number.

14

Circle it on the number line.

| 1 | 2 | 3 | 4 | 5 | 6 | 7 | 8 | 9 | 10 | 11 | 12 | 13 | (14) | 15 | 16 | 17 | 18 | 19 | 20 |

Show it in the twenty frame.

| O | O | O | O | O | O | O | O | O | O |
| O | O | O | O | | | | | | |

Fill in the missing numbers.

| 11 | 12 | **13** | **14** | 15 | 16 | **17** | **18** | 19 | **20** |

Thursday: Number Talk

Answers vary. Students have to pick numbers and discuss the addition facts with their neighbors. They should prove they are correct. For example, students might say 5 and 5 are ten and model it with their fingers.

Friday: Make Your Own Problem

Answers vary. They can model with a drawing, a number line, a ten frame.

Week 6

Monday: Always, Sometimes, Never

This is a reasoning routine. Students have to choose what they think and then give examples to prove that they are correct. In this case, it is sometimes.

Tuesday: Alike and Different

Students should talk about how they are both solids. Answers vary. For example, both solids have 1 curved surface. One solid has a vertex and the other solid doesn't.

Wednesday: How Many More to 10

5 – 5 more
7 – 3 more
3 – 7 more

Thursday: Number Talk

The conversations should focus on what happens when you take a number from itself. Students should work with different models to see it.

Friday: Model It

$2 + 8 = 10$

Students should draw a picture and model it in the ten frame. Students should draw a picture and model it in the ten frame. Also have them discuss the count on strategy so that they know to start with 8 and count up 2 to solve this problem.

Week 7

Monday: What Doesn't Belong?

The quadrilateral does not belong.

Tuesday: Alike and Different

Students discuss how these shapes are alike and different. For example they talk about how all of them have closed straight sides. They talk about how all of them have vertices. They should also talk about how 2 of them have 4 sides.

Wednesday: Number Bond It!

Students have to reason about numbers. They should fill in the number bond and discuss why it is correct.

6 and 1
2 and 5

Answers vary.

Thursday: Number Talk

Students should discuss and model what happens when you take zero away from a number. For example, 5 − 0 equals 5.

Friday: Problem Solving

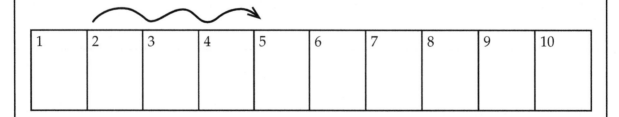

Whole 5	
Part 2	Part 3

1	2	3	4	5	6	7	8	9	10

Week 8

Monday: True or False?

Students should talk about how this is true because it has 6 sides, 6 angles and 6 vertices. They should then discuss other types of hexagons as well.

Tuesday: Vocabulary It Is/It Isn't

Rectangle

It Is	It Isn't
A shape Has 4 sides 2 long sides 2 short sides Straight sides 4 vertices (corners)	Doesn't have curved sides Isn't wavy Isn't open

Wednesday: Number Bond It!

Answers vary. For example:
1 and 8
2 and 7
3 and 6
4 and 5
0 and 9

Thursday: Number Talk

Answers vary. Students have to pick 2 numbers. Make a subtraction problem. Describe how they solved it.

Friday: Model It

○ ○ ○ ○ ○
○ ○

○	○	○	○	○
○	○			

$7 - 2 = 5$

Week 9

Monday: Convince Me!

Students have to use different ways to show that $4 + 6 = 10$. They can use their fingers, objects, number lines, ten frames and act it out.

Tuesday: Vocabulary Talk

Students discuss that compose means to build it and decompose means to break it apart. They should give number examples. For example, $2 + 3 = 5$ is to compose 5. If they have 5 and break it apart they can say $5 = 4$ and 1. Illustrate this with number bonds.

Wednesday: Guess My Number

6

Thursday: Number Strings

Students should talk about the count back strategy and how we can use it when we see a 1,2, or 3.

Friday: What's the Story?

Answers vary.

Students should tell a story about the picture.
For example: There were 3 ladybugs and 5 butterflies. How many animals were there altogether?

Week 10

Monday: Convince Me!

Students should talk about how they can make 8 by either adding or subtracting. They should discuss how you can model it in many ways.

Tuesday: Vocabulary Talk

Students discuss the words sum and difference. They should give specific examples. For example, sum is the answer to an addition problem like 3 + 3 = 6. 6 is the sum. Difference is the answer to a subtraction problem like 4 − 2 = 2. 2 is the difference.

Wednesday: Number Of the Day

17

Write the number: 17	Part- Part Whole		Twenty Frame
	17		O O O O O O O O O O
	10	7	O O O O O O O

Circle the ones that make 17: (8 + 9) (17 + 0) 5 + 5 10 + 17	Solve: 17 + 1 = 18 17 − 1 = 16	How many more to 20? 3

Twenty frame:

(twenty frame with 17 filled squares and 3 empty squares)

Thursday: Number Talk

Students should talk about doubles facts.

$1 + 1 = 2$ $2 + 2 = 4$ $3 + 3 = 6$ $4 + 4 = 8$ $5 + 5 = 10$

Friday: What's the Question? (3 Read Protocol)

Answers vary. How many more yellow crayons are there than green ones? How many crayons are there altogether?

Week 11

Monday: Reasoning Matrices

Students have to reason about the problems.

Sue ate the chocolate chip cookie. Carl ate the heart cookie. Lucy ate the cookie with sprinkles.

Tuesday: Vocabulary Bingo

The focus is on teen words. Students put the numbers in the boxes. Then the teacher should show number bonds, part-part whole mats and describe numbers in tens and ones and show visual representations to play bingo. Students cover the number and whoever gets 3 in a row wins.

Wednesday: Greater Than, Less Than, in Between

Students work on sequencing the numbers. They use the number line or hundred grid to think about the numbers. Answers will vary.

What is a number that is greater than 3? **4 or 5**	What is a number that is less than 10? **9 or 7**	What is a number that is greater than 20? **28, 22**
What is a number that is less than 3? **1 or 2**	What is a number that is in between 3 and 10? **4 or 8**	What is a number that is in between 10 and 20? **11 or 17**

Thursday: Number Talk

Students subtract and then discuss their strategy.

Friday: Problem Solving

Students have to discuss what the different combinations could be.

Chickens	Cows

Week 12

Monday: Legs and Feet

A. 6.
B. 2 cows and 1 chicken; 1 cow and 3 chickens.

Tuesday: Vocabulary Brainstorm

Answer vary.
Students should write about subtraction using numbers, words and pictures.

For example, take away, minus sign, $7 - 1 = 6$.

Wednesday: What Doesn't Belong?

$25 - 1$

Thursday: Number Talk

Students should discuss that we can count up or back. We could also use our Make Ten friends fact to think about this problem.

Friday: Equation Match

1. $4 + \_ = 10$

Week 13

Monday: What Doesn't Belong?

Students reason about what goes together and what doesn't.

A. Difference B. 3 + 2 +3

Tuesday: Frayer Model

Answers vary.

Equation

Definition	Examples
A number sentence with an equal sign	$4 + 1 = 5$
When do you use them?	**Non-examples**
Word problems	$4 + 7$

Wednesday: Compose It!

Students work on representing numbers in a variety of ways. Answers vary.

6 and 0
5 and 1
4 and 2
3 and 3
2 and 4
1 and 5

Thursday: Number Talk

Students should discuss when numbers sit side by side on the number line that they have a difference of 1. We can count back or to find the answer. They should be able to explain that the answer is the number that comes just before the number we are subtracting from.

Friday: What's the Story?

Students work on modeling word problems with different tools. They should tell a story about this picture. For example: There were 3 elephants and 4 giraffes came. How many animals are there now?

Week 14

Monday: Always, Sometimes, Never

Not always, if you subtract 0 the number stays the same.

Tuesday: Vocabulary Bingo

Students should explain the shape to their math partner.

Wednesday: Guess My Number

A. 18.
B. 27.

Thursday: Number Talk

Students should give examples of doubles facts and discuss how they help us to add by using them.

For example, 2 + 2, 4 + 4 or 5 + 5.

Friday: What's the Story?

Answers vary. For example:

1. There were 7 lollipops. Jan ate 1. How many are left?
2. Draw model.
3. 7 − 1 = 6.

Week 15

Monday: How Many More to

Start at 2 Add 10
Start at 3 Add 9
Start at 4 Add 8
Start at 5 Add 7
Start at 6 Add 6
Start at 7 Add 5

0   20

*Students should discuss the pattern. They should also discuss different ways to figure these problems out like doubles, doubles plus 1 and bridging 10.

Tuesday: Vocabulary Fill-in

A. Sum.
B. Difference.
C. Addend.

Wednesday: What Doesn't Belong?

A. 14–7.
B. 9 + 1.

Thursday: Number Strings

Students should discuss that taking tens away you have to adjust the tens column

Friday: Problem Solving

A.

Whole 8	
Part	Part
?	3

B. ? + 3 = 8

Week 16

Monday: Reasoning Matrices

Carl loves football.
Lucy loves soccer.
Sue loves baseball.

Tuesday: Vocabulary Bingo

Answers vary. Students have to discuss the numbers out loud.

Wednesday: Missing Numbers

		23	24	25	
31	32	33		**35**	
	42			45	46

Thursday: Number Talk

Answers vary. For example, 2 + 2 is 4. I did it in my head. It's a doubles fact.

Friday: Model It

There is 1 more butterfly than ladybug.

Week 17

Monday: Missing Numbers

Kelly is correct. 10 would not make sense because it would mean $13 = 7$ which is not true.

Tuesday: Vocabulary Bingo

1 + 1 double	10 − 5 half fact	8 − 1 count back	7 + 2 count on
9 + 0 add 0	9 + 3 count on	5 + 5 doubles	2 − 0 take away zero
6 + 1 count on	4 + 4 doubles	1 + 1 doubles	7 − 2 count back
5 + 3 count on	8 + 2 make ten	5 − 3 count back	2 + 2 doubles

2 + 2 doubles	10 − 4 think ten friends	7 − 1 count back	6 + 4 make ten
6 − 0 take away zero	9 + 3 count on	5 + 2 count on	8 + 0
5 − 2 count back	9 + 1 make ten	8 + 2 make ten	6 + 2 count on
3 + 3 doubles	5 + 5 doubles	4 − 3 take away 1	4 + 4 doubles

Wednesday: Greater Than, Less Than, in Between

Answers vary.
Write a number greater than 15. **16**
Write a number less than 92. **91**
Write a number in between 34 and 41. **35**

Thursday: Number Talk

Answers vary. $1 + 9$; $2 + 8$; $3 + 7$; $4 + 6$; $5 + 5$.

Friday: What's the Question? (3 Read Protocol)

Answers vary. How many fruits are there altogether? How many more apples are there than bananas?

Week 18

Monday: True or False?

A. True.
B. False.
C. Answers vary.

Tuesday: What Doesn't Belong?

A. Circle.
B. 8 – 4.

Wednesday: Guess My Number

A. 18.
B. Answers vary.

Thursday: Number Strings

Students should discuss what happens when you add 10 to a number. The value in the tens place changes.

Friday: Problem Solving

6 fish.

Week 19

Monday: How Many More to

Start at 10 … How many more to 20? **10**

Start at 15 … How many more to 20? **5**

Start at 18 … How many more to 20? **2**

Tuesday: Vocabulary Bingo

4 – 1 count back	3 – 0 zero fact	4 – 4 take away a number from itself	9 – 1 count back
9 – 2 count back	7 – 6 neighbor numbers	10 – 10 take away a number from itself	10- 2 think ten friend or count back
4 – 2 count back	10 – 4 think ten friend	5 -5 take away a number from itself	5 – 0 zero fact
8 – 7 differ-ence of 1	7 – 7 take away a number from itself	5 – 3 count back	10 – 7 think ten friend

8 – 8 take away a number from itself	7 – 2 count back	5 – 1 count back	10 – 2 think ten friend or count back
10 – 10 take away a number from itself	5 – 1 count back	8 – 2 count back	7- 6 neighbor numbers
0 – 0 zero fact	3 – 0 zero fact	9 – 8 neighbor numbers	2 – 0 zero fact
6 – 5 neighbor numbers	2 – 2 take away a number from itself	10 – 5 think ten friend	6 – 3 count back

Wednesday: Number Bond It!

Answers vary.

$1 + 11$, $2 + 10$, $3 + 9$, $4 + 8$, $5 + 7$, $6 + 6$

Thursday: Number Talk

Answers vary.

Friday: What's the Story?

Answers vary. There were 10 cats and 7 ran away. How many cats are left? **3**

Week 20

Monday: True or False?

	True or False?
$5 + 10 = 5 + 5 + 5$	True
$12 - 8 = 8 + 4$	False
$10 = 5 + 5$	True
$5 - 5 = 0 - 0$	True
Make your own!	Answers vary

Tuesday: Vocabulary Brainstorm

Answers vary. Students should write about doubles, illustrate doubles and give examples of doubles.

Wednesday: What Doesn't Belong?

Answers vary.

A. rectangular prism.
B. $10 - 7$.

Thursday: Number Talk

Answers vary. Students should discuss taking away neighbor numbers. They should discuss how they have a difference of 1 because they sit side by side on the number line.

Friday: Problem Solving

There were 5 more fish than turtles.

Week 21

Monday: Missing Numbers

$3 - 3 = 0$

$1 - 1 = 0$

$10 - 10 = 0$

Tuesday: Vocabulary Talk

Answers vary.

Wednesday: Number Bond It!

Answers vary.

Students represent numbers in a variety of ways.

$7 + 7$; $8 + 6$; $2 + 2 + 10$.

Thursday: Number Talk

Students discuss what happens when you take 10 away from a number.

Answers vary. For example: $20 - 10 = 10$.

Friday: What's the Story?

Answers vary. There were 5 dogs. 2 more came. How many dogs are there now? **7**

Week 22

Monday: True or False?

True.

Tuesday: Frayer Model

Difference

Definition	Examples
The answer to a subtraction problem.	$2 - 2 = 0$ $10 - 7 = 3$
Give a Picture Example 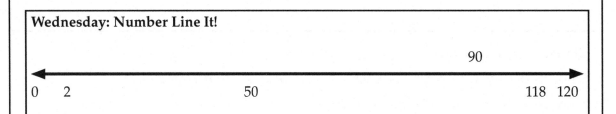 $5 - 3 = 2$	Non-examples $5 + 4$

Wednesday: Number Line It!

```
                                         90
<--------------------------------------------------->
0    2                    50                  118  120
```

Thursday: Number Strings

What happens when you add 9 to a number. You want students to focus on bridging through 10. For example, $9 + 3 = 9 + 1 + 2$.

Friday: What's the Question? (3 Read Protocol)

Answers vary.
How many rings does she have altogether? How many more yellow rings does she have than pink ones?

Week 23

Monday: Magic Square

8	1	6
3	5	7
4	9	2

Tuesday: Frayer Model

Compare

Definition	Examples
To discuss how things are the same and how they are different.	She has 4 marbles and her sister has 2 more than she does. How many does her sister have?
Give a Picture Example 5 is more than 4	**Non-examples** 5 + 4

Wednesday: Number of the Day

18

How many tens? 1 How many ones? 8	Base 10 sketch ○ ○ ○ ○ ○ ○ ○ ○
Twenty frame	Answers vary. $10 + 8 = 18$ $19 - 1 = 18$

Thursday: Number Strings

Students should discuss how they can use the ten friend strategy to help solve subtraction problems where you are taking a number away from 10.
For example, $10 - 7$ think $7 + ? = 10$. The answer is 3. So, $10 - 7$ is 3.

Friday: Problem Solving

Students work on solving word problems with different models.
3 were turtles.

Week 24

Monday: Reasoning Matrices

Sue is on the slide. Lucy is on the swingset. Marvin is on the monkey bars. Carl is on the seesaw.

Tuesday: Vocabulary Quick-Write

Answers vary. Students should write about how addition is joining things together. For example, they can talk about the plus sign, give an example of an addition equation or draw a picture.

Wednesday: Number Line It!

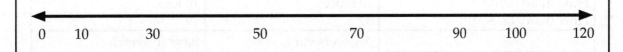

| 0 | 10 | 30 | 50 | 70 | 90 | 100 | 120 |

Thursday: Number Talk

Answers vary. For example:

$50 - 30 = 20$

$90 - 50 = 40$

Friday: Model It

There were 8 ladybugs.

Week 25

Monday: What Doesn't Belong?

A. 30 – 30.

B. 8 + 8.

Tuesday: Alike and Different

Answers vary. For example, 16 and 61 are both 2 digit numbers. 16 is less than 20 and 61 is more than 20. They both have a 6, but the 6 in 16 is worth 6 ones and the 6 in 61 is 6 tens.

Wednesday: Number of the Day

20

How many tens? 2 How many ones? 0	10 more 30	10 less 10
<table><tr><td>Ten</td><td>Ones</td></tr><tr><td>2</td><td>0</td></tr></table>	Answers vary. _____ + _____ = 20	Base 10 sketch

Thursday: Number Strings

Students should discuss what happens when you take away 9 from a number. For example: 14 – 9 They should think about bridging back through 10 meaning 14 – 4 = 10 10 – 5 = 4 or 14 – 10 + 1.

Friday: Make Your Own Problem

Answers vary.
Students work on solving word problems using a variety of models.

Week 26

Monday: Always, Sometimes, Never

Sometimes. When you add 0 the number stays the same.

Tuesday: Frayer Model

Answers vary.

Cube

Definition	Examples
It is a 3D figure with squares on all 6 sides.	It looks like a box.
Give a Picture Example Dice	**Non-examples** A triangle, a circle

Wednesday: Compose It!

Answers vary. $1 + 7$; $2 + 6$; $3 + 5$; $4 + 4$.

Thursday: Number Strings

Students should talk about bridging 10 or taking away 10 and adding 2 back.

Friday: What's the Story?

Problem B.

Week 27

Monday: Magic Square

2	7	6
9	5	1
4	3	8

Tuesday: It Is/It Isn't

Cone

It Is	It Isn't
rolls curved 3D it stands	2D flat on all sides a polygon

Wednesday: Greater Than, Less Than, in Between

Answers vary.

99 108 120

Name a number less than 99: 67	Name a number greater than 108: 109	Name a number less than 120: 101
Name a number greater than 99: 102	Name a number in between 99 and 108: 100	Name a number in between 108 and 120: 112

Thursday: Number Strings

Students should talk about how these are half facts.

Friday: What's the Story?

Answers vary.

Sue had 4 marbles. She got 1 more. How many does she have now?

Students work on solving word problems with a variety of models.

Week 28

Monday: Missing Numbers

Fill in the missing numbers on the piece from a hundred grid.

51	52	53	54	**55**	56	57
61				65		
71				75	76	77

Tuesday: Vocabulary Fill-in

Name some number words that you know.

When you add a number to itself it is a <u>doubles</u> fact.

<u>Equal</u> means "the same as".

The answer to an addition problem is the <u>sum</u>.

The answer to a subtraction problem is the <u>difference</u>.

The <u>addend</u> is one of the numbers you add in an addition problem.

Wednesday: Legs and Feet

A. 6.
B. Answers vary. There could be 2 ducks and 2 turtles or there could be 1 turtle and 4 ducks.

Thursday: Number Talk

Students should talk about how you can count back or count up or bridge ten.

Friday: What's the Problem?

Maria has 4 marbles. Her sister has 2 more than she does. How many does her sister have? Her sister has 6 marbles.

Week 29

Monday: Magic Square

6	1	8
7	5	3
2	9	4

Tuesday: Frayer Model

Sphere

Definition	Examples
A solid figure with 1 curved side	Orange, globe, ball
Give a picture example	Non-examples
	Triangle, square, cone

Wednesday: Number of the Day

Answers vary.

57

Base 10 sketch	57 is greater than 50
⏐⏐⏐⏐⏐ ○○○○○○○	57 is less than 70
Tens 5 Ones 7	$57 + 10 = 67$ $57 - 10 = 47$

Thursday: Number Talk

Answers vary. $7 - 7 = 0$.

Friday: Model It

$4 + 6 = 10$

○○○○ + ○○○○○○

Ten Frame

○	○	○	○	○
○	○	○	○	○

Week 30

Monday: 3 Truths and a Fib

10 < 7

Tuesday: Vocabulary Brainstorm

Answers vary. Students should discuss how geometry is about shapes. They should name some shapes and draw some shapes.

Wednesday: Number Line It!

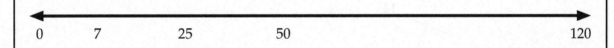

25   7   120   50

0   7   25   50   120

Thursday: Number Strings

Students should talk about the relationship between doubles and half facts.

Friday: What's the Question? (3 Read Protocol)

Answers vary. For example: How many did they have altogether? How many fewer lemon cookies did they have than chocolate chip ones?

Week 31

Monday: 2 Arguments

Maria was correct because 8 + 2 makes 10.

Tuesday: Vocabulary Match

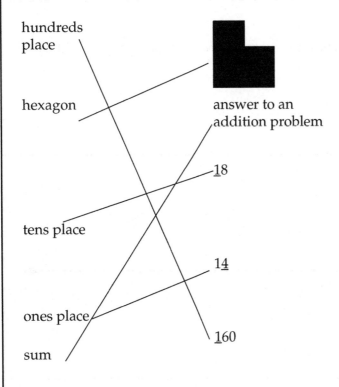

hundreds place

hexagon

tens place

ones place

sum

answer to an addition problem

1_8_

1_4_

_1_60

Wednesday: Alike and Different

Answers vary. Some examples include:

Alike	Different
Both have the digit 2 Both larger than 10 Both have the digit 1	The 2 in the 12 is worth 2 ones The 2 in the 120 is worth 2 tens 120 is larger than 100 12 is less than 100

Thursday: Number Talk

Students should be discussing bridging up or back through ten.

Friday: What's the Story?

Answers vary. For example: There were 5 dogs and 2 more came. How many dogs are there now? 7   5 + 2 = 7

Week 32

Monday: Graphs

Answers vary.
How many dogs are there?
Which animal got the most votes?
Which animal got the least votes?

Tuesday: Vocabulary Match

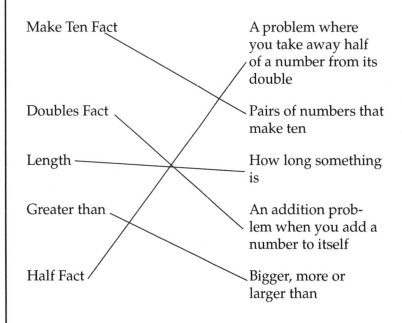

Make Ten Fact	A problem where you take away half of a number from its double
Doubles Fact	Pairs of numbers that make ten
Length	How long something is
Greater than	An addition problem when you add a number to itself
Half Fact	Bigger, more or larger than

Wednesday: Convince Me!

Both sides equal 10 so it is true.

Thursday: Number Talk

Answers vary. For example, $18 - 9 = 9$.

Friday: Equation Match

The bakery had 10 cookies. They made some more. Now they have 12 cookies. How many did they make?

Week 33

Monday: What Doesn't Belong?

6:30

Tuesday: Vocabulary Match

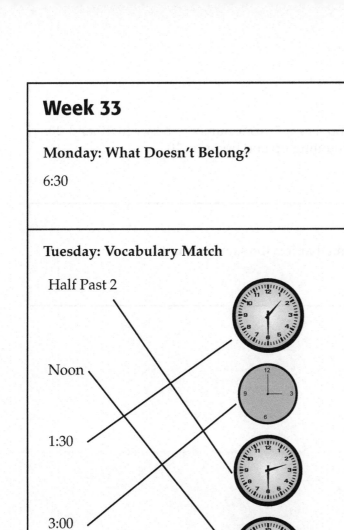

Half Past 2

Noon

1:30

3:00

Wednesday: Number of the Day

100

Number line it	Write the number
0 ←——————→ 100	100
Base 10 sketch	Answers vary
	100 is greater than 50.
	100 is less than 900.
	100 is the same as 10 tens.

Thursday: Number Strings

Students should discuss strategies for subtracting 7 from numbers between 10 and 20. They should focus on partial differences, counting up and bridging 10.

Friday: Model It

Grandma is correct. Students should explain that it is the same amount.

Week 34

Monday: Reasoning Matrices

Sue likes horses. Lucy likes pigs. Marvin likes cows. Carl likes sheep.

Tuesday: Vocabulary Match

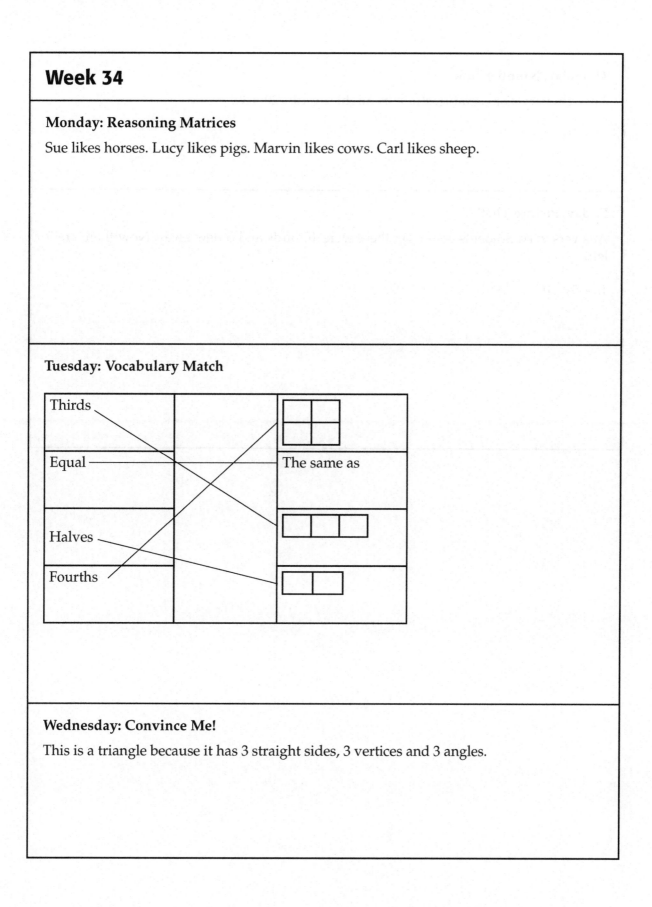

Wednesday: Convince Me!

This is a triangle because it has 3 straight sides, 3 vertices and 3 angles.

Thursday: Number Talk

Answers vary. For example, students might say $10 + 20 = 30$.

Friday: Picture That!

Answers vary. Students could say there were 10 birds and 5 flew away. Now there are 5 left.

$10 - 5 = 10$

Week 35

Monday: True or False?

True. It has 6 sides, six angles and 6 vertices.

Tuesday: Vocabulary Tic Tac Toe

A.

4	10	7
1	8	5
10	8	10

B.

0	3	2
3	1	2
5	2	1

Wednesday: Number Bond It!

Answers vary.

9 + 10   11 + 8   20 − 1

Thursday: Number Talk

Answers vary. Counting back or counting up.

Friday: Make Your Own Problem

Answers vary.

Week 36

Monday: Missing Numbers

Answers vary. $5 < 7$ $4 = 2 + 2$ $10 > 1$

Tuesday: It Is/It Isn't

Answers vary.

50

It Is	It Isn't
A 2 digit number Greater than 40 It is less than 100	A 1 digit number Greater than 60 It Is It Is Not Less than 10

Wednesday: Greater Than, Less Than, in Between

Answers vary.

Name a number greater than to 82	Name a number less than 110	Name a number less than 100
84	100	99
Name a number greater than 110	Name a number in between 82 and 110	Name a number in between 100 and 110
120	100	101

Thursday: Number Talk

Answers vary. Students should talk about counting up or making it a 10 and subtracting 2. For example, 74 + 8 could by 74 + 10 – 2.

Friday: Equation Match

The answer is A.

Week 37

Monday: How Many More to 20

Start at 10 ... How many more to 20? **10**

Start at 11 ... How many more to 20? **9**

Start at 15 ... How many more to 20? **5**

Tuesday: Vocabulary Bingo

9 − 1 Count back	3 − 0 Zero fact	4 + 4 doubles	9 − 9 Take away a number from itself
9 − 2 Count back	7 + 3 Ten friend	10 − 9 Neighbor number	10 − 2 Think ten friend
8 − 3 Count back	10 + 0 Add zero	10 − 5 Half fact... think doubles	5 − 0 zero fact
8 − 7 Neighbor numbers	7 − 7 Take away a number from itself	5 − 3 Count back	10 − 7 Think ten friend

9 − 9 Take away a number from itself	5 − 2 Count back	7 + 2 Count up	10 − 5 Think ten friend
7 − 7 Take away a number from itself	5 − 1 Count back	8 − 2 Count back	6 − 3 Half fact ... think doubles
0 − 0 Zero fact	10 − 5 Half fact think ten friend	9 − 8 Neighbor numbers	4 + 4 Doubles
6 − 5 Neighbor numbers (difference of 1)	8 + 0 Add	7 + 3 Ten friend	6 − 3 Count back

Wednesday: Guess My Number

A. 110.

B. 18.

Thursday: Number Talk

Answers vary. These are all doubles plus 1 facts so you want students to think about how doubles could help them.

Friday: What's the Story?

His brother has 10 marbles.

Week 38

Monday: Graphs

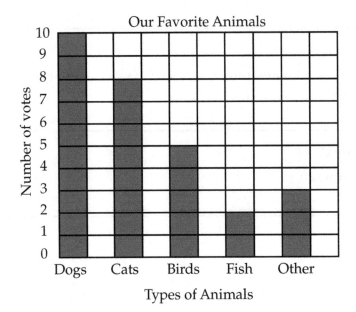

Our Favorite Animals

Answers vary: How many people voted? Which animal got the most votes? How many more people liked dogs than cats?

Tuesday: Vocabulary Tic Tac Toe

Students have to discuss the word with their partner. They have to draw or write or explain their thinking before they put the x or o. Whoever gets 3 in a row first wins.

Answers vary.

Wednesday: Missing Numbers

Answers vary.

$5 + 5 > 4 + 4$

Thursday: Number Talk

Answers vary. Students should focus on bridging 10.

Friday: Problem Solving

Answers vary.

Week 39

Monday: Graphs

Our Favorite Pies

Strawberry	☺ ☺ ☺ ☺ ☺ ☺ ☺
Lemon	☺ ☺ ☺ ☺
Apple	☺ ☺ ☺ ☺ ☺
Other	☺ ☺ ☺

Answers vary. For example:

How many people voted?
What was the most liked flavor?
What was the least liked flavor?

Tuesday: Vocabulary Tic Tac Toe

Students have to discuss the words with their partner. They have to draw or write or explain their thinking before they put the x or o. Whoever gets 3 in a row first wins.

Answers vary.

tens	Hundreds	Plus sign
equation	Equal sign	Minus sign
ones	Less than	Greater than

triangle	rectangle	square
cylinder	circle	cube
hexagon	hexagon	trapezoid

Wednesday: Number Line It!

Answers vary.

Thursday: Number Talk

Answers vary. For example, $7 + 6$ or $11 - 2$.

Friday: Model It

Joel ate more.

Week 40

Monday: Reasoning Matrices

Sue likes the elephant. Carl likes the zebra. Lucy likes the giraffe. Marvin likes monkeys.

Tuesday: Vocabulary Tic Tac Toe

Students have to discuss the word with their partner. They have to draw or write or explain their thinking before they put the x or o. Whoever gets 3 in a row first wins.

Answers vary.

Fourths	Halves	Thirds
Fraction	Quarter	Whole
One-fourth	A third of	Half

Wednesday: Magic Square

Students had to fill in the squares so that adding them in any direction made 18.

3	10	5
8	6	4
7	2	9

Thursday: Number Talk

Answers vary.

Friday: What's the Question?

Answers vary. For example: How many more lemon cookies did it have than sugar ones? How many fewer sugar cookies did it have than lemon ones?